The Dog Diet

The Dog Diet

KATE BENDIX

Published in 2016 by
Short Books, Unit 316, ScreenWorks,
22 Highbury Grove,
London, N5 2ER

10 9 8 7 6 5 4 3 2 1

ISBN: 978-1-78072-250-4

Cover design: Two Associates
Cover image of dog ref: 150048 © Stocksy
Cover image background and bowl ref: 357367 © Stocksy
Cover image food in bowl ref: 184322590 © Getty
p.27 Body conditioning score table layout: Kevin Green

Printed at CPI Group (UK) Ltd, Croydon, CR0 4YY

For Nikita
Rescue dog, tripe-lover, best friend

Contents

Foreword

In 1973 when I embarked on my career as a vet, I knew quite a lot about how to treat illness in dogs, and I have learnt a lot more over the last forty plus years. But at the time I never gave much thought to the diet my patients were being fed. Vets didn't sell pet food or give much advice on feeding. You got your dog's food from a pet shop, or bought green tripe from the butcher and mixed it with offcuts and scraps from home.

Most dogs were pretty healthy on the whole; most of my work was treating infections and carrying out surgery. Gradually, I noticed an increasing number of dogs with persistent eczema, inflammatory bowel disease, under-active thyroid, diabetes and other chronic, long-term conditions.

In recent years there has been a veritable tidal wave of such cases. Coinciding with this tsunami of chronic disease in dogs has been a massive increase in the incidence of obesity in dogs.

The first thing I now do when I meet a new patient with any persistent health problem is to ask about diet.

If, as is mostly the case, the answer is kibble, or a low-grade canned diet, I suggest that unless the diet is improved, any treatment I give will not be sufficient to make a major difference. And if the client explains that the food is purchased from the local vet (who now has a waiting room stacked from floor to ceiling with bags of kibble) I have to bite my tongue to refrain from saying what I really think!

So – if diet is so important, what is the best way to feed a dog? How can you stop your dog becoming obese? What are healthiest foods, treats and supplements? Can you feed your dog a home-cooked diet? Why is kibble a no-no? How do you make sense of the ingredients on pet food labels? Are there natural ways of avoiding fleas and worms? Is raw feeding safe?

The answers to all these questions, and more, are in *The Dog Diet*. Kate Bendix has somehow managed to pack into this small volume an amazing amount of superbly useful and – above all – practical information, all in a clear, concise and very readable way.

I tend to rate books on the lettuce scale. Cos (too big and too long), or Iceberg (too dense and boring) Or, like *The Dog Diet* – a Little Gem!

Dr Richard Allport, BVetMed, VetMFHom, MRCVS
Natural Medicine Centre
www.naturalmedicinecentre.co.uk

Introduction

We have known for decades now that what we eat is crucial to our own long-term health. If we eat poorly – a diet high in processed carbohydrates, processed meat, ready-meals and sugar – the pounds will start to pile on. We'll feel tired and sluggish, with achy joints added for good measure. And we know that, if we carry on eating this way, we're heading for chronic diseases further down the line: diabetes, heart disease, cancer, inflammatory bowel disease and skin problems.

On the other hand, if we eat a variety of foods, freshly sourced and prepared, and we limit our intake of sugar and carbs, we are likely to remain slimmer and fitter, to sleep better and have more energy. We are what we eat, and, even if we've got ourselves into a middle-aged state of being overweight and lethargic with aching knees (me) we know that by changing how we do things it can all go away and we can stave off chronic, life-shortening disease. (Also me. Lost a stone so far. Yay, go me!)

Unsurprisingly, the same logic applies to our dogs. Millions of them are porkers. Their lives have come to mimic our own – too many of them are over-fed, under-exercised and stressed – and so it stands to reason that they have started to take on our shape and disease pattern. Over the past 20 years the rise in obesity, diabetes, heart disease, cancer, inflammatory bowel disease and skin problems in our dogs has rocketed. Now compare this list to the one above. Notice any similarities?

The truth is we dog owners *are* sometimes guilty of over-feeding our beloved dogs and perhaps not always feeding them the right things. But we are also the victims of an onslaught of marketing misinformation, which has made it increasingly difficult to know what on earth a healthy canine diet actually looks like. We have grown up feeding our dogs processed cans and kibble, for example, because we believed the myths put about by the food companies: 'Stick to one food, don't deviate' (utter rubbish); 'grain-free is best' (is it, really?); 'developed with vets' (I don't even know what that sentence means).

Luckily, help is at hand. There is enough nutritional advice in this book to put a stop to your dog's weight gain and reverse the downward trend in her health. A good dog diet is not rocket science, I promise you. And it won't cost you a fortune, or eat into your precious down time. More to the point, your dog will love it. So let's learn from ourselves and help our dogs back to health.

Chapter 1

How we got here

Doggy dysmorphia

Now I'm not saying you, or your dog, is fat, I wouldn't dare to presume. But, with 62% of men and women in the UK in 2014 being overweight or obese I'm guessing that some of you reading this book are. I am, and I'm writing the thing, for crying out loud!

The problem is that most of us just don't recognise our dogs for what they are: fat. We are doggy dysmorphic, blinkered. In our mind's eye our dog is hurtling through the tall grass that sways in the warm summer breeze. Her coat is sleek and glossy, she has a waist Audrey Hepburn could only have dreamt of and a set of teeth white enough to make an A-lister weep. Meanwhile, back to reality… if we carry on the way we are going, just five years from now the number of overweight dogs in the UK will outweigh (sorry!) the number of healthy dogs. The simple truth is we are in denial.

If the vet tells you your dog is overweight, in your head

they are being critical and you hear, 'You are a failure, your dog is overweight, what were you thinking?' You feel guilty, and as if you've lost control, which brings on denial and self-loathing. The denial and self-loathing then trigger the same action that made you feel bad in the first place – overfeeding your dog – and the degradation continues. Now you're in a shame spiral. It's a cycle that repeats itself over and over.

You can't beat Denial, though; it's a great destination. All cosy, dark and snuggly like a posh spa, without the relaxing music. Nothing bad ever happens in Denial. That's because nothing ever happens at all! If you heave the dog on to the vet's table only to be told, 'Ms Smith, if Millicent is ever to see her feet again she needs to lose weight,' it feels like a personal attack, as if you let your dog get into this state on purpose. So we stick our fingers in our ears, sing a happy tune and deny, deny, deny. Whereas if we choose to hear it and *most importantly* not beat ourselves up about it, then we can finally take action.

Why do we overfeed?

Apart from re-fuelling, for many of us eating is a pleasurable experience. Feeding our dogs is equally pleasing – a loving thing to do. We project our emotions around food and the pleasure it gives us on to our dogs. As we graze, so shall they. A passing piece of cheese here, what's left at the bottom of the Weetabix bowl there... It becomes a habit. We sit on the beach with our fish and chips and the dog gets a bit. It's Saturday, she looks at you with those soulful eyes and gets half your toast and jam. It's a regular thing, another bond between you, sharing toast of a morning. I can hear you saying that they only get the odd *this* and the occasional *that*, but to a small animal that's a big deal.

This is especially true if you think about how rarely we tend to 'scale up' what we're feeding our dogs. For instance, a digestive biscuit is to a 10kg dog what seven digestives is to a 70kg human. That's not something you just eat in passing. If a 10kg dog needs approximately 600 calories a day and a plain digestive contains 73 calories, one digestive is more than ⅛th of the daily ration.

Equally, we aren't exactly renowned for sticking to the feeding guidelines on a packet of dog food. How many times have you doled out the recommended amount, and then thought to yourself, 'Well that doesn't look like much!', before dishing out a little more...? And yet even if we *are* following the guidelines, it's estimated that we could be overfeeding our dogs by anything between 10-60% a day because dogs as a species vary so much. Are you starting to get the picture? It isn't looking good, is it?

Guilt is also a huge factor in overfeeding our dogs, and it's exhausting. You feel guilty for leaving them alone while you go to work; guilty for having to go out some nights; guilty when you realise it's been three hours and all you've done is stare at your tablet with one eye on the TV while the dog slept next to you and you could have taken her for a walk or played a game. So you slip her an extra treat or two. The guilt can feel relentless.

What Marketing Man knows

Somewhere along the line, it has become acceptable to feed our dogs the same meal, day in day out, for years. A dog lives, on average, to be 12 years old. We feed him twice a day. That's 8760 meals over his lifetime. To avoid wasting money, and so as not to upset our dog's digestion, once we find a food our dogs like, at a price we are happy to pay (on average 50p per day per 12kg dog), we tend to stick with it.

It's then the pet food marketers' job to get us to deviate; to try and ensure that as much money as possible goes into Pedigree's pocket (owned by Mars) as opposed to Baker's (owned by Purina/Nestlé).

The psychology around what makes us buy one packet of dog food over another, and how we choose to feed our dogs throughout their lives, is quite complex. Feeding the dog triggers a powerful emotional and nurturing response in us. We want the best for them, of course we do. We want to get that happy wagging tail by the food bowl and feel we've done our job well.

Marketers know this and use these responses and desires to stack the odds against us. So we don't choose what to feed our dog all on our lonesome. We have help! Sadly, what we're told is often not what we're actually sold. Put another way, the food you choose to feed your dog might not be as healthy as you have been led to believe it is. Words like 'natural' and 'hypoallergenic' are widely abused and can be misleading.

Marketers are smart and know they need to get you early. Research shows that once an owner commits to a pet food brand, they are likely to stay with it – through thick and thin, or should that be thin and thick? So new owners are particularly vulnerable. They don't have the first clue about what to feed a puppy when they get one, so they will probably go for a brand they've already heard of, or for one recommended by their breeder (and guess where they get *their* information from?)

So you've got your favourite pet food brand, and you dutifully add it to your shopping trolley every week, safe in the knowledge that it has come highly recommended, it has always gone down well and certainly hasn't caused any notable harm. But then you start to notice that your dog is putting on weight, and has that unique doggy whiff about her, and you're so confused you start in on the pet forums, seek help from the vet (who's on a nice whack from a multinational like Mars) or other dog owners – and we *always* have an opinion. All this just melts your brain. But don't worry, Marketing Man is here to support you. In fact Marketing Man is ubiquitous and he'll have you up and running on 'the right thing' in no time. Silly woman (yes, it is more often than not women who buy the dog food, so the message is tailored specially for us). There, there, make us a cuppa while I slide a 12kg bag (with 2kg extra free!) of I Can't Believe It's Actually Dog Food (with Added Happiness) into your trolley.

One pet food consultant I spoke to says he feels very sorry for dog owners. Manufacturers know to play to our emotions and so very few foods have nutrition at the core of what they do. 'They don't get me so easily,' I hear you shouting. Yeah? Then ask yourself these questions: why do you buy the pet food and treats you do? Of what benefit do you think they are to your dog? Do you buy it for their health or for your convenience? Are you swayed by claims on the packet such as 'hypoallergenic' or 'natural'? This doesn't make you an idiot, it makes you a human being with a conscience – and Marketing Man loves you for it.

'Wackaging'

A mash up of wacky and packaging, wackaging is a way of marketing which makes everything 'such fun'! Or, in the case of dog food marketing, such natural, wholesome, everything-in-the-garden-is-rosy fun. That can of food you're serving up? From the picture on the side, you'd think it was lovingly prepared by the WI in a church hall kitchen. Now you can pay twice the price! Ladies and gentlemen I give you pet food which states it is 'slow cooked', 'lovingly made', a 'hotpot supper prepared in our factory kitchens'. Whichever way you come at it – whether you're buying the cheap and nasty or the super premium – you're getting tucked up like a kipper, my friend. The trouble is that as long as a pet food reaches the minimum nutritional standards to be classed as a 'complete food', and the ingredients and analysis are clearly listed on the back of the packet, the marketers can say what they like – barring any health claims they can't back up. 'Dogs love meat!' 'Dogs will do anything for those meaty chunks.' Who knew?

Selling dog food is no different to selling anything else. It's all about your emotions and the guilt if anything should go wrong on your watch: baby products 'give them the best start'; cars 'keep your family safe'; dog treats with added joint supplements will 'turn him into a puppy again!' Bluergh, someone pass me a sick bag.

And in the spirit of no niche ever going unfilled, now that our dogs are getting fatter those lovely marketing bods at Blah Blah Blah Plc. have created a range of diet foods aimed squarely at the rapidly expanding (I couldn't help myself) overweight dog market. This is where we started with human food in the Sixties with low-fat yoghurt and slimline bread. Anyone remember the Nimble girl? Flying high in a hot air balloon? It's 50 years later and we are at that point with dog food.

If we humans had just carried on eating our meat and fish, fruit and veg with the odd treat thrown in, and not eaten so much of it, we'd have given the obesity epidemic the swerve. Let's reverse the obesity trend in dogs while it's still a relatively new thing.

Education is key

How are you supposed to know what to do if no one teaches you? One of the biggest obstacles in tackling our dogs' diet is that many of us don't know how to feed *ourselves* properly, let alone our dogs.

Teaching kids to cook in school, I mean really cook, as a life skill, went out of the window years ago. So the next generation of mums and dads had no knowledge to pass on. Cue the big food companies with ready-meals or 'ping dinners', as my friend Matt likes to call them, robbing us of even the most basic cooking skills and, bingo, here we are, not two generations on, our knowledge of what nutrition actually is and how it affects our bodies eroded. And this, in one of the richest countries on earth. Shame on you successive governments for giving in to the food lobbyists. Look at what most of your NHS budget goes on treating now: diabetes. You're reaping what you sowed only a few scant years ago.

I was shopping in my local supermarket recently, earwigging on other people's conversations, as one is inclined to do when standing, bewildered, in an aisle dedicated entirely to pasta, when I overheard a conversation between a young couple who had clearly recently moved in together and were out doing their weekly shop. Unfazed by the overwhelming choice of shapes and sizes of pasta on display, they were busily shovelling packets of the stuff into their trolley when she said, 'We need to get some of that low-carb pasta sauce.' It was just a casual, throwaway instruction but one that left me breathless at just how messed up our understanding of food now is.

Let me get this straight – a *low-carb* pasta sauce to mix through a plate of almost pure *carbohydrate*? Excuse me?

Precisely the same thing has happened to our pets, only it's *worse*. This is because, not only do we feed our dogs almost entirely on prepared, shop-bought dog food, never deviating or adding variety, we don't really know what constitutes the good stuff.

Our feeding choices should always have the dog and its long-term health at the forefront, and for this we should not be relying on the supermarkets or marketers to guide us. In the end you have to decide what kind of dog owner you want to be. The one who spends time learning about their dog's dietary needs and reacts accordingly by shopping around for great dog food, watching what they eat and how much exercise they get; or the one who takes the path of least resistance and ends up spending way more in the long run on their dog's diabetes and arthritis treatment.

Some of this is about self-control. I watched a TV

programme on life in a zoo recently. I'd never considered what all the different animals ate on a daily basis before or what a job that must be for whoever managed the zoo's kitchen. Turns out the zoo has a full-time nutritionist employed to look after the welfare of their furry, feathery, leathery charges and he must take everything about their lives into account before working out what to feed them. Species, activity levels, age, boredom, etc, are all considered before recipes, methods and timetables for feeding are made up for each animal.

The zoo nutritionist made a really interesting point that's stuck with me. He said, 'These animals are in such good condition because of what we feed them. If we were in there and they were out here and could eat all they like, we'd be the ones in amazing shape. They [pointing to a honed-to-perfection group of tigers] would be fat because they could eat what they wanted. They're not programmed any differently from us.'

Wow. This could be the new craze – the 'Zoo Diet'. Lock me up and hide the key for six months. Feed me what I need, only when I need it, and let me lounge about on a rock the rest of the day picking my feet, only moving occasionally to sidle up to a group of unsuspecting visitors and show them my backside, just like a chimpanzee. 'Does my bum look big in this? Oh no, I forgot, I've lost two stone!'

We say we want the best for our dogs, but our walk and our talk are at odds with one another. It's there in black and white, in the PDSA Animal Welfare (PAW) report of 2014,[1] a survey of vets, vet nurses and pet owners which makes for a sobering read.

It states that: '86% of pet owners believe owning a pet improves their lives, and four out of five pet owners feel physically or mentally healthier because of their pet.' So they make us feel better, give us company and comfort, and make us happier people.

It goes on to say that the large majority of pet owners are aware of obesity-related health issues such as diabetes, heart disease and arthritis and 88% acknowledge that overweight pets will have a 'shortened lifespan'. It then says that even during the recession, pet owners did not reduce their spending on preventative care for their pets. We love our mutts and even when times are hard we are willing to pay whatever it takes to make our sick dogs well again because they bring so much to our lives.

Yet a lot of the money we spend on preventative health-care could be saved with one simple change: keeping our pets' weight down. A healthy diet has been proven to significantly reduce and delay the need for long-term medication and to prolong a dog's life by up to three years.[2]

There is no love in cake

There is no question that we love our pets because they

bring so much to our lives. And yet we're letting them get fat even though we know, in our heart of hearts, it will make them sick. Love in itself is not enough. Love will not stop their digestion suffering, their pancreas packing up or their joints disintegrating under the ever-increasing weight and pressure of the extra lard they're carrying about. Only a good diet and exercise will give them a healthy life.

To summarise, we overfeed our pets for the same reasons we overfeed our loved ones or eat too much ourselves:

Emotional responses – We associate food with love and to feed someone is to love them.

Those damn hormones – When we look into the eyes of someone we love, especially children, our brain releases the 'love' or bonding hormone oxytocin. The same thing happens when your dog looks at you with those big brown eyes. Both you and your dog release oxytocin. The longer the look lingers, the more oxytocin is released.

We're busy and inherently lazy – Modern life has its pressures and when we come home from work, we're too late/busy/tired to cook for ourselves, let alone make a special trip to the pet shop to buy better food and treats for the dog

We live in fear and lack confidence – Decades of mental pummelling by advertisers have eroded our confidence and we no longer trust ourselves to make good choices.

Marketing – Marketers are fully aware of all the reasons above and push the same buttons they use to sell us baby formula, junk food and 'functional' foods which will make us 'better', i.e. yoghurt with 'good' bacteria in it. (God help us!)

To overfeed and eat too much is in our DNA. And, just as we human beings have begun to acknowledge that we are what we eat, and what we eat isn't doing us any good, we must accept that the same is true for our dogs.

We need to wake up and smell the gravy. Cast denial aside and wise up. Having a healthy and happy dog is easy, I promise you. That's what this book is all about.

Chapter 2

What you need to know

First things first, let's find out if your dog is overweight. Use the Body Conditioning Score table on the right to get an idea. It works for every dog and is widely used by pet professionals. The key to using it is to be brutally honest with yourself about your dog's shape. No one's watching, or judging. Close the curtains if you like.

Rather than thinking about his weight, you're looking at the shape of your dog. So, stand behind him. Place both of your thumbs on either side of his backbone. Now, spread both hands across his rib cage. The ribs should be easy to feel under the coat without excessive fat covering – like pens in a soft pencil case.

Now, stand back and look at him from the side and from above: can you see his waist? Feel your dog's belly. Run your hand underneath from the end of the chest along the belly, it should follow an upward curve and not droop downwards. This is known as the abdominal tuck.

How did he do? Ideally your dog should have a Body Condition Score (BCS) of 3 (or just under if you have

WHAT SHAPE IS YOUR DOG?

A little extra weight can be a **BIG PROBLEM.** Whether it's once a month, once a week or once a month, check your dog's body score regularly to make sure he's staying happy and healthy.

BODY 1 SCORE
VERY THIN
<5% body fat

Ribs
Easily felt with no fat cover

Tail Base
Bones are raised, no fat cover

Side View
Severe abdominal tuck

Overhead View
Accentuated hourglass shape

20% below ideal body weight

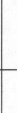

Consult your veterinarian!

BODY 2 SCORE
UNDERWEIGHT
5-15% body fat

Ribs
Easily felt with little fat cover

Tail Base
Bones are raised with slight fat cover

Side View
Abdominal tuck

Overhead View
Marked hourglass shape

10% below ideal body weight

Consult your veterinarian to see if you are underfeeding your dog

BODY 3 SCORE
IDEAL BODY WEIGHT
16-25% body fat

Ribs
Easily felt with slight fat cover

Tail Base
Some contour with slight fat cover

Side View
Abdominal tuck

Overhead View
Well-proportioned waist

Ideal body weight

Great job!
Keep doing what you are doing

BODY 4 SCORE
OVERWEIGHT
26-35% body fat

Ribs
Difficult to feel under moderate fat cover

Tail Base
Some thickening, bones palpable under moderate fat cover

Side View
No abdominal tuck

Overhead View
Back is slightly broadened at waist

10% above ideal body weight

Consult your veterinarian about the right nutrition for your dog and about ways to increase activity

BODY 5 SCORE
OBESE
>35% body fat

Ribs
Difficult to feel under thick fat cover

Tail Base
Thickened and difficult to feel under thick fat cover

Side View
No waist, fat hangs from abdomen

Overhead View
Back is markedly broadened

20% above ideal body weight

Extra weight can cause serious health problems for your dog. Consult your veterinarian about the right nutrition for your dog.

a leaner breed – a greyhound or lurcher, for example). Remember you are being honest with yourself. Denial has no place here. If your dog is too thin or too fat, ask your local vet for advice. They will look for any underlying health problems. If there aren't any, it's time for them to eat better and move more. It's Boot Camp for Butch!

I should say here that most vet practices run free weight clinics for pets, which are a great resource. However, the majority of vets receive incentives and commissions from pet food companies. They also have sales targets to meet. Don't be fooled: you don't have to buy their recommended diet food to take part. Just take the weight checks and the advice, and make the necessary changes yourself.

The impact of an unhealthy diet

Now for a little science. Until recently, the cells that store fat in our bodies, known as adipose tissue, were thought to be just that, a fat store. However adipose tissue is now widely accepted to be an endocrine organ in its own right.[3] The endocrine system releases hormones into the blood, which travel all over the body and set to work.

When dogs are a healthy weight these hormones keep the body in a stable state known as homeostasis. But when a dog gains weight, the hormones start to have an inflammatory effect, which over time can have an impact on the dog's whole physiological system: heart, pancreas, liver, kidneys and immune system. This is the starting point for a host of chronic diseases, including diabetes, heart disease, and cancers. They also happen to be the three main life-shortening conditions that affect dogs, i.e. the big killers. And we're not talking about morbidly obese pets here. Studies have shown that even moderately over-weight dogs are at risk of early death.[4]

If you have a short-nosed, broad-headed breed: a pug, Cavalier King Charles Spaniel, Chihuahua or Bulldog for example, putting on weight entails further complications. Because of their particular shape, breathing, eating and swallowing can be challenging for these dogs even at a healthy weight. Excess weight can lead to severe respiratory distress, including brachycephalic syndrome, an upper airway problem that in serious cases can cause dogs to collapse or faint after exercise because they aren't getting enough oxygen. Other symptoms include coughing, gagging, retching and vomiting, especially in hot weather.[5]

The conditions brought on by an unhealthy weight are upsetting to witness and eye-wateringly expensive to treat. When an average dog becomes diabetic, after initial diagnosis she will need: insulin and needles at £75 per month (these figures are from my vet practice and they're very reasonable); three-four visits every ten days until her insulin levels have stabilised and you're confident about how much insulin to administer every day; and three visits a year thereafter to make sure her pancreas is stable.

Every visit clocking in at £30-£40 a pop.

To give you an idea, a 12kg dog with diabetes is going to cost £1100 per year just to manage the disease. Consider too that a lot of pet insurance policies now only cover a single illness for up to a few thousand pounds and impose an unrealistic time limit of a year per condition after which they will not pay out. Is the picture becoming clearer? A little bit of cheese, or an extra handful of kibble is a short-term win for your dog with long-term, expensive and painful consequences for everyone.

Clearly not all overfed dogs go on to develop full-blown diabetes, but an unhealthy diet can cause a whole host of other common problems:

- Wind/flatulence
- Bad breath
- Allergies
- Blocked anal glands
- Loose stools
- Constipation
- Poor coat condition
- Itchy skin
- Candida (yeast overgrowth)
- Lack of energy and concentration
- Too much twitchy energy
- That classic doggy smell

Many of you will recognise some if not all of the problems listed above. They're the sort of common ailments that us dog owners know as part and parcel of daily life – those niggling, can't-quite-put-your-finger-on-why-they're-happening health problems that come and go, despite one's best efforts. But fret not, because pretty much all of them can be fixed or managed with a change of diet.

Think of your dog's digestion as a pipeline: food, treats, water, supplements, drugs, bits of paper, glitter go in; numbers 1 and 2 come out. What goes in is reflected not only in what actually comes out: wind, diarrhoea, that gelatinous, bloody horror show known as colitis, but also in outward symptoms: itchy skin, gunky eyes and ears, blocked anal glands, greasy fur. All this is a reflection of the health of your dog's gut, and changing to the right diet can work wonders.

Case study – Debbie

Seven years ago we rescued an 18-month-old Cairn Terrier who turned out to have the most horrendous skin allergies. Her skin problems have cost me a fortune in 'remedies' and vet bills over the years, I hate to think… A year ago, I caved, and put her onto Apoquel tablets from the vets – for the first time in her life Daisy had an itch-free summer.

Then, in November I had her tested for allergies and discovered that Daisy had not only a grain intolerance, but was allergic to all types of protein except chicken protein. And these allergies had manifested themselves in itchy skin. So that's when I switched to a diet of Forthglade grain-free chicken dog food, Laughing Dog wheat-free mixer and home-cooked vegetables. Needless to say, Daisy doesn't need the tablets anymore and is itch-free! Not to mention the weight she's lost and bundles of energy she's gained. It was a relief to find out that a change in diet was all that was needed and that itchy skin didn't have to be the status quo.

Make a health wishlist

Like Daisy, does your dog have any persistent issues or problems? Write down anything that comes to mind and put it somewhere safe. You're going to refer back to this later. If your dog has any serious health problems – diabetes, long-term steroid use, arthritis – put that at the top. Next, if your dog is overweight, write that down and try and remember when the weight problems started. Finally, add any other health or behavioural concerns you have: smelly ears, itchy paws, excess energy, stiff joints, etc.

Whatever changes you make to your dog's current regime as a result of reading this book, will need some time to take effect. Hang on to this list so that you can return to it to see what has improved. I know you'll be pleasantly surprised. You may even find yourself gobsmacked.

What your dog needs

Dogs need a balanced and varied diet. There is good research to show that in a healthy dog, a low carbohydrate, high protein, fruit and vegetable diet is the way to go.[6] And in my view, the best way to achieve this is a mixture of shop-bought wet food, raw food and home-cooked grub – more on this in the next chapter. The beauty of this approach is that once you've got your dog to a satisfactory weight you won't need to worry so much about portion control to ensure they maintain it. It just works.

But let's not get ahead of ourselves. For most of us, figuring out the ideal amount to feed our particular dog is a real headache.

This may sound like no-brainer, but it's worth spelling it out: you can't rely on your dog to work out how much food he needs per day. This is because Fudge's instinct is to consume as much as he can whenever he gets the chance; he is biologically programmed to prepare for food shortages – only the food keeps coming. He isn't hungry, but it's just not in his nature to walk away when there is still food in his bowl.

Feeding guidelines on dog food packaging are equally misleading. Think of them as mere estimates. For the past decade or so, the consensus has been that a dog needs to consume 2-3% of her bodyweight daily, which takes into account metabolism and activity level. This equates to feeding a 10kg dog between 200g and 300g. An ambiguous figure at best.

A study published in 2014 stated that, 'estimating energy requirements [for pets] based on bodyweight alone may not be accurate'. So far so confusing! Unsurprisingly, the study found that dogs with a higher level of activity needed more calories, while dogs classed as having low activity levels (i.e. one hour per day) needed on average only 62 calories per kilo of bodyweight per day. The study also found that, puppies aside, age and sex don't affect the energy requirement of a dog, but being neutered definitely does. A neutered dog may need as many as 25% fewer calories per day.

So what is a dog owner to do? I was mulling this over and came to the conclusion that the ambiguity actually frees you up to take matters into your own hands. You've used the Body Condition Score and you've thought about any niggling health problems it would be great to get sorted. Now be honest with yourself about your dog's activity levels: how many times a day do you go for walks? Is your dog neutered? All these factors will affect how much he should eat.

For the nerdier owners among you who would like to be a bit more formal about it, go to thedogdiet.co.uk where you will find a handy calculator. Just put in your dog's size, and a few answers which you'll find on the back of your dog's food packet, and it will work out how much of that food he needs. As I say, there is no exact science to this but, that will give you a starting guide at least.

For everyone else, the simplest way of assessing your dog's needs is to work out how much he is currently eating per day (in grams). If you feed your dog by eye and don't know what her current intake is, simply measure out his normal amount of food, then weigh it.

If your dog is a healthy weight, you can stick to his current intake. If your dog is overweight, then you need to give him less – read on!

The magic number

I'm now going to offer a very simple rule of thumb for achieving sustained and gradual weight loss (of between 3-5% of your dog's bodyweight per month).

Here's how you do it. Take the amount that your dog is currently eating per day (in grams) and reduce that figure by approximately 15%. Let's say your dog weighs 12kg, but she should weigh 10kg, and her current intake is 400g of food per day, without treats. If you're making the 15%

reduction on her current 400g, that's 60g less food per day than you would normally feed, i.e. from now on you're going to feed her 340g per day. Just to be clear, this figure is not an accumulator, it's a one-off calculation, and 15% is the maximum reduction you want, no more.

Now remember this is still an estimate, but it's a very solid starting point. This is something you literally have to keep an eye on. See if her weight rises, falls or stays the same, and move on from there. If your dog starts to look a little heavy or her harness is getting a bit tight, put her on the scales. If you're walking past the vet's, take your dog in to get weighed on the big scales. Use the Body Conditioning Score periodically, get used to how those ribs and tucked-in belly should feel. No one knows your dog better than you. I check Nikita daily as I'm stroking her. It sounds over the top but it's second nature now, a subconscious thing. Weigh your dog and take measurements if you like, let's make it a challenge.

IMPORTANT: Always get your dog checked over by your vet before reducing her food intake.

DOUBLY IMPORTANT: Don't ever starve your dog or restrict intake by more than 15% in an attempt to make him lose weight quickly. You want your dog to lose weight gradually while still getting the right balance of nutrition. Losing weight is about changing eating habits and instigating a lifestyle change and will take time. It's the tortoise not the hare that wins in this race. Isn't it always?

Nutrition is everything

Whatever you're feeding your dog it is essential to get the balance of nutrition right. If you're DIY-ing it, make sure you're using really fresh food – don't wing it. Using shop-bought dog food means the nutrition is already added for you, so what you're looking for is a great list of ingredients, excluding any which might cause upset.

The chart below gives you an idea of what vitamins and minerals should regularly feature in your dog's diet and why:

Food	Vitamins and minerals	Benefits
Lean meat and fish	B vitamins – thiamin B1, riboflavin B2, niacin B3, B6 and B12	Building and preparing tissue. Hair and nails are mostly made of protein. Builds bones, muscles and cartilage
Green, leafy veg, asparagus, cauliflower, courgette, cucumber, corn (off the cob), celery, peppers	Vitamins A, C and K and folate. Minerals – iron and calcium	Good for heart health, bones, kidney function and immunity
Sweet potato, carrots, swede, turnips	Vitamins A and C, beta-carotene, potassium	Good for the immune system, blood pressure and nerve impulses, healthy skin and teeth
Peas, barley, quinoa, broad beans and green beans	Potassium, phosphorus, calcium, B vitamins, iron and calcium	Good for energy levels, healthy nerves, heart, muscles, a healthy immune system and building red blood cells

Food	Vitamins and minerals	Benefits
Seaweed	Vitamins A, B, C. Minerals – calcium, iodine, potassium, magnesium	Nails, coat condition. Kills bacteria which cause plaque and tartar build up
Apples	Fibre, vitamin C	Good source of fibre, vitamin C helps protect immune system, helps digestion (can help with diarrheoa)
Bananas	B6, manganese, vitamin C, copper, fibre and potassium	Good source of fibre and potassium, helps treat diarrheoa, good for maintaining proper heart function and regulating normal blood pressure
Watermelon – seeds removed	Thiamin, riboflavin, niacin, vitamin B6, folate, pantothenic acid, magnesium, phosphorus, potassium, zinc, copper, manganese, selenium, choline, lycopene	Coat condition, eye health. Lycopene has been linked with helping asthma sufferers
Strawberries	Vitamin C, fibre, antioxidant-polyphenol, manganese, potassium	Lowers blood pressure, excellent source of vitamin C, which helps protects against immune system deficiencies, good for eyes, lowers cholesterol
Blueberries	Vitamins C & K, manganese, fibre	Protection against illness, keeping up immunity
Cranberries	Vitamins C, E & K, fibre, manganese, pantothenic acid	Helps prevent UTIs, good for immune system, good anti-inflammatory

Food	Vitamins and minerals	Benefits
Raspberries	Vitamins C, E & K, manganese, pantothenic acid, biotin, magnesium, folate, omega-3 fatty acids, potassium	Good for bone strength, kidney function and immunity
Pears	Fibre, vitamin B2, C & E, copper, potassium	Helps lower cholesterol levels, high in fibre, helps prevent high blood pressure
Oranges – seeds and peel removed	Vitamins C, B1, A, pantothenic acid, folate, calcium, copper, potassium	Vitamin C helps protect immune system, good to help maintain cholesterol levels
Honey	Vitamin B6, pantothenic acid, calcium, copper, iron, magnesium, manganese, phosphorus, potassium, sodium, zinc	Boosts energy, local honey may help tackle allergies. Good for skin condition and immunity
Peanut butter	Vitamin E, magnesium, folate, copper, phosphorus, fibre, manganese	Good source of protein. Good for skin health and slow release energy
Brown rice	Vitamin B6, magnesium, phosphorus, selenium, thiamin, niacin, manganese	Selenium helps reduce cancer risk. Good for mopping up toxins in the body and normalising cholesterol levels
Eggs* *(the occasional egg, shell and all, is a perfect all-in-one food)	Essential fatty acids and calcium	Good for bones, joints teeth and hair

The trick is to make sure you get a variety of all these ingredients to achieve the balance of nutrients your dog needs. For example chicken contains high levels of phosphorus – essential for healthy bones, teeth and nails – and niacin which is vital for converting carbohydrates into energy. Oily fish, like salmon, mackerel and sardines, contain high levels of vitamin A – important for healthy skin and eyes – and also essential fatty acids, Omega 3 and 6, which the body can't make for itself. These help to regulate the metabolism, reduce inflammation throughout the body, and are important for brain function.

Foods to avoid

It's crucial you learn what dogs can't eat. Some human food is downright dangerous for dogs. They can eat raw chicken, we can eat raisins and grapes, but confusing the two can kill you both!

Dogs don't eat like we do, they don't digest food the way we do and they hardly *ever* spit anything out. While there is a wide range of human food that is safe and beneficial for dogs to eat, there is quite a long list of foods that they are very sensitive to. These can be so harmful that they should definitely be kept out of reach:

Food	Ingredient	Effects
Chocolate	Theobromine and caffeine	Seizures, heart arrhythmia, death
Alcoholic drinks	Alcohol	Depression of central nervous system – slows respiratory rate, can be fatal
Onions	Thiosulphate	Damages the red blood cells – anaemia
Raisins and grapes	Not known	Diarrhoea, lethargy, dehydration, kidney failure
Cooked bones		Can splinter, causing obstruction and/or lacerations in the mouth, throat and stomach
Avocado	Persin – a fungicidal toxin	Stomach upset. The avocado stone can cause obstruction if swallowed
Coffee, tea, cola and energy drinks	Caffeine	Seizures, heart arrhythmia
Milk/yoghurt/cream	Lactose	Dogs can be lactose intolerant – stomach upset, diarrhoea, itchy skin
Macadamia nuts	Not known	Pain for up to 48 hours, fever, weakness in the back legs
Sweets, chewing gum, diet foods, toothpaste	Xylitol	Rapid drop in blood sugar caused by increased insulin release. Disorientation and seizures, liver failure
Fat trimmings from meat	Fat	Pancreatitis, liver and kidney problems
Soft fruit stones in peaches, plums, cherries	Cyanide (peaches and plums)	Inflammation of the small intestine, obstruction, poisoning
Sweets, sugary food and drinks	Sugar	Obesity, bad teeth, diabetes

Food	Ingredient	Effects
Processed foods – cured meats – crisps and salty snacks	Salt	Excessive thirst and urination. Not good for the kidneys. Can cause seizures

A brief word on carbs

I'll stick my neck out and wager that a few of you reading this will have tried the zero-carb Atkins diet at some point. If you managed to stick to it I bet you lost a shed load of weight. I did. How long did it take you to put it all back on again, however? For me, it was about a year. While following this type of diet slavishly will make the weight drop off, for most of us it's not sustainable, and there is research to show we can damage our heart and kidneys by eating mostly protein over the long term. It's exactly the same story for our pets.

They need carbs, but it's important to differentiate between good and bad ones – even for dogs. Complex carbohydrates are very healthy. Their nutritional benefits are legion: providing slow-release energy; aiding digestion; helping regulate metabolism; improving sleep; keeping the immune system strong, and the nervous system in shape. Complex carbs come from unprocessed, or whole foods: fresh vegetables, fruit, brown rice, quinoa, whole oats, pearl barley and sweet potato for example.

However, 'bad', or refined carbohydrates wreak havoc

on the pancreas, insulin levels and endocrine systems, leading to lethargy, obesity, diabetes, heart disease and arthritis. Refined carbohydrates are basically anything processed and on the beige end of the colour spectrum: refined flours, sugar, crisps, sweets, biscuits, cakes – and dry dog food!

So I say this with conviction in my heart; as much as possible – and it *is* entirely possible – ditch the dry food. Even if it's top notch kibble, it doesn't matter how good the carbohydrate source was when it started out, by the time it's gone through the cooking process it has become a refined carbohydrate. A dog food version of Kellogg's finest if you will.

When I ask a pet owner what they're feeding their dog, they often say, 'Hardly anything and she's still putting on weight, and begging for food!' Well if she's only eating kibble, this doesn't surprise me. As we shall see, it's not always about the *amount* of food a dog is getting, it's what that food consists of. The refined carbs in kibble cause insulin levels to shoot up fast, and then plummet just as speedily, so the dog ends up in a sugar trough, desperate for more.

My cat Pearl was not only obese, but quite often sick until I got her off the kibble, and on to a diet of good wet food and home cooking. The Catkins Diet! She was six and heading for diabetes and an early death. She will be 15 this year and doesn't have a weight problem (only an attitude problem, but she's always had that!). She gets her carbs from fruit and vegetables and from food that I cook for her.

But for three-quarters of the dogs in the UK, dry dog food, or kibble, is all they will ever eat, which is why so many of them are overweight or obese, and suffering identical diseases to us. No one is asking you to start knitting your own yoghurt, not overnight anyway! But it is as well to understand the difference between good and bad carbs and to avoid refined carbs as much as possible. And if you need any further convincing, hear this:

Uncooked carbohydrate

One ingredient that is really going to irritate your dog's gut is raw starch. You might think it's absent from your dog's diet, but it hides in uncooked carbohydrate – in, yes you've got it, kibble! Raw starch can be harmful to your dog because the bad bacteria in the gut thrive off it and these then overwhelm the good bacteria, leading to all sorts of problems, from bad breath and wind to colitis and skin problems.

Most dry food is made by extrusion, a process unchanged in decades. The ingredients are mixed together then cooked under steam and pushed through an extruder (a giant corkscrew/meat grinder type affair.) An extruder works using friction, which builds heat. It cooks carbohydrates, turning them from raw starch into a digestible gelatinised form.

Dry food recipes these days are higher in protein and fat content and lower in carbohydrate content than they were a few years ago. You'd think that this would be good news, except that it means that the extruder doesn't cook the carbs as thoroughly and they remain only partly gelatinised. Most producers aim for a 95% cook but if you get below an 80% cook – meaning 20% of the starch is raw – this can have a significant impact on your dog.

To test for uncooked carbs, put a small handful of kibble in a bowl, cover it in hot water and leave it for 20 minutes. The kibble should absorb all the water. When it has cooled, squeeze the paste together to wring out the moisture; the mixture should be completely soft with no hard bits left, and the kibble should remain intact, not turn to porridge. If there are any hard bits left behind, you should consider changing foods as this is evidence of raw starch which will be causing a proliferation of bad bacteria in your dog's gut. Another way to check is to snap a piece of kibble in half. You should be able to see all the little holes where the starches have cooked through. Uncooked starch is denser and very biscuit-like.

In my dreams I want to hear the sound of kibble rattling its way out of packets and into bins all over the land. But, of course, I know this isn't realistic, and that there are those among you who can't afford the luxury of simply cutting out all dry food in favour of wet food or home-cooking in one fell swoop. I just ask you to bear in mind the kibble test, and in the next chapter I will return to this to give you some useful pointers on how to separate the good dry-food brands from the bad.

Case study – Sharon

We have a three-year-old Jack Russell Terrier called Wilma. She is full of life and is a bright little character, but at about six-nine months old she started being sick quite a lot. She was always scratching her face and gums, and we couldn't work out what was wrong. We took her to the vet and she told us Wilma was allergic to pollen, and prescribed some antihistamines. They reduced the itching but didn't stop the sickness.

Wilma then started to lose weight quite fast and began to look very thin. One vet told us to run a blood test to determine what she was allergic to, the next told us that such tests are often inconclusive. So we decided to do our own research. I had recently spoken with a lady who said her dog was allergic to all grains, even rice, and when I trawled the Internet I found it was quite a common problem among dogs with sensitive digestion.

I searched for the best rated grain-free dog food and landed on Canagan, which is nearly 60% animal protein, with sweet potato and peas as carbohydrates – no wheat, maize or rice.

We weren't sure whether Wilma or our other dog, Freddie, would eat the dry food as they were used to wet food. The petshop owner told us to warm the bowls slightly or put the food in the microwave for ten seconds to release the aroma. We tried the microwave thing for a week and they loved the food; they still do. It took about ten weeks for Wilma to become well again. Thank goodness we made the change. Both our dogs seem much healthier (you can always tell by what comes out the other end!). Wilma still has her pollen allergies, but we keep the itching to a minimum with Piriton once a day and a splash of Yumega Plus, and a good wipe down after she has been running in grass.

Repetition, repetition, repetition

As mentioned earlier, it has become commonplace to feed our dogs the same food for years on end. This lack of variety can be a problem in itself. Unsurprisingly, dogs are becoming intolerant to certain food groups and there is growing evidence that Adverse Food Reaction (AFR)[7] is on the rise. AFR is caused by an intolerance to ingredients that are continuously served up. This is particularly true of chicken, because it's practically the only protein modern dogs ever get their jaws around. AFR rarely leads to a full-blown food allergy, but it puts the sufferer 'on alert' which can lead to chronic itchy and dry skin, flea-allergic dermatitis, leaky gut, colitis – nice things like that. When these conditions persist, they compromise your dog's immune system and wear her down, not to mention causing you worry and incurring a small fortune in treatment. Luckily, they're the kind of problems you can easily clear up with a varied diet.

In summary

- Reduce your dog's current intake of food by 15% – no more than that – and watch for gradual weight loss of 3-5% of his bodyweight. He'll look marvellous.
- Cut down on the kibble; if possible, cut it out completely. The process by which dry pet food is produced involves refining the carb content. Refined carbs play havoc with your dog's blood sugar levels and irritate his gut.
- Introduce more variety into his diet. This will increase the nutritional content of his food, keep his tastebuds fizzing, and reduce the likelihood of food intolerances. Happy days.

Chapter 3

How to feed your dog

There are three ways to feed your dog: you can give them commercial (shop-bought) food, raw food, or home-cooked food. In this chapter we will be looking at all three methods in turn. You can go for one or two of these methods, or for a combination of all three (which is what I practise and preach). In the next chapter, I give you my top raw and home-cooked recipes, including healthy treats and even a healthy doggy birthday cake (serves 4).

Whatever and however you decide to feed, you are looking to achieve an overall balance of nutrition through variety, and a diet that works for *your* dog. Dogs need the right mix of proteins, carbohydrates (the good ones), fats, fibre, vitamins and minerals in their diet. They also need high-quality ingredients, which can be difficult to find in today's price-conscious market. (More on this later.)

As we saw at the end of the last chapter, exposing your dog to as many foods (which are safe for dogs to eat) as possible is a good thing as she is less likely to develop a food intolerance.[8] In fact, adopting a trial-and-error approach has the added benefit of you being able to identify an ingredient which might be disagreeing with your dog. Say for example she has long suffered from flatulence. In an attempt to get to the bottom of it, you switch brands. Bingo, your house is a fart-free zone at last! It may be that the canned food you used to feed her contained poor-quality vegetable by-products which, unbeknownst to you, weren't doing her any favours. This may sound obvious, but I promise you that the majority of dog owners, once they have settled on a brand, will stick to it pretty much forever more. I cannot stress this enough: variety is best.

Each type of food – commercial, raw and home-cooked – has it advantages and disadvantages. Let's dissect each feeding method one by one and weigh up the pros and cons.

Commercial or shop-bought food (wet and dry)

Pros
- Safe and highly regulated
- Nutritionally balanced
- Convenient
- And cost effective (most of the time)

Cons

- Often poor-quality nutrition
- It's very easy to overfeed
- Repeated use of the same food can lead to intolerances and adverse food reactions
- Labelling can be confusing and misleading

The myth of the 'super-premium' brand

In the UK, £2 billion's worth of pet food is bought every year. Unsurprisingly, nearly 90% of that figure is spent on household names and own brands bought at the supermarket. Convenient, remarkably well priced and always in stock, big brands are often the obvious choice. But because they're made to as low a price-point as possible, the food quality and nutritional value can be pretty awful.

In recent years, rising labour, energy and ingredient costs have meant it is very difficult to make money on economy foods, so many companies have developed high-end lines known as 'super-premium' brands, which have seen rapid growth. This rise has been further fuelled by how saturated the pet food market has become. Producers find it increasingly hard to stand out from the crowd, and everyone is looking for the next point of difference.

But exactly how 'high-end' are the super-premium brands? The short answer is: often, not very. In processing terms, these ostensibly up-market efforts are very similar to most economy foods. New products are designed to fit into standard processing methods, not the other way around. It's just too expensive to develop new manufacturing processes and equipment in order to retain more of a food's original nutritional value, especially if it's possible to add it in later.

That said, whether it is super premium or Tesco's own brand, commercial dog food in this country has to fulfil multiple criteria. It must meet the minimum nutritional standards set out by The European Pet Food Industry Federation (FEDIAF). It must be palatable to the dog; affordable, available and consistent for the owner. And, as far as the retailer is concerned, it must be able to live on a shelf at room temperature for 18 months or so without spoiling. As the saying used by overworked people everywhere goes, 'Shall I put a broom up my bottom and sweep the floor as I go?' Furthermore, these standards are applied to the foodstuff of a mammal which has the greatest diversity across its species. A Chihuahua can weigh as little as 1kg, but this is a mere snack weight to a dog at the other end of the scale, a 150kg Mastiff!

A side note: prescription dog foods, designed to tackle a particular problem – kidney disease or struvite stones – are not disingenuously described, they *are* carefully formulated. However, foods that claim to be breed-specific, size-specific, age-specific, or to target issues such as poor digestion, are simply not what they say they are.

The differentiating factor that you're looking for when choosing a shop-bought food is the quality of the ingredients. But how can you tell one over the other when a can of dog food costing £1.20 could be just as good in the ingredients department, if not better, as another costing £2.40? I'm exhausted just reading this back to myself.

What to look for

Time to separate the good from the bad and the just plain ugly. With dog food, you can legitimately hark back to the 'good old days' in some cases. Arden Grange, for instance, is still making some of the best food out there because they're conservative and don't follow trends. They formulated a dog-food range 25 years ago when nutrition was at the heart of good grub and their recipes haven't changed much since. Here are my top tips when buying commercial dog food:

Buy British – Without doubt the Brits make the best pet food in the world. We use the best ingredients and have the most up-to-date manufacturing equipment. So, ask food producers where their food is made. Any imported pet food must be checked by DEFRA upon entry into the country, but since they are now as under-resourced as everyone else in the public sector, policing and inspections of imports is not what it was. As a rule of thumb, the richer the country the better the quality of the ingredients they put into their pet food, and whatever you think about the state of the nation, we are far from broke.

Aim for a good balance of ingredients – Commercial dog food is going to suit a lot of dog owners, particularly those who don't have the time to cook or the freezer space to store raw food. Whether you prefer kibble or wet food (that's your dog's preference, not yours), what you're looking for is a mix of: fresh meat or meat meal, a poultry-based fat, good carbs, vitamins and minerals.

Note how the ingredients are listed – It's the first six ingredients which really count, so as a rule of thumb, any ingredient that appears on a packet or tin after the first six is there for marketing purposes only. Food supplements, such as glucosamine and chondroitin, are an exception. They must be listed as an 'additive' rather than an ingredient. Make sure they come after food (e.g. carrots) and before any vitamins or minerals. If the first six ingredients are followed by a long list of fruit and vegetables, remember this: producers buy a 1kg pack of fruit and veg which they add to 1 tonne of food. So if carrot is listed as the seventh ingredient it's probably present in minute amounts (like 0.1%). In shop-bought wet and dry food, these are the sorts of ingredients lists you want to see:

Great shop-bought wet food	Great shop-bought dry food
Chicken (65%)	Prepared de-boned chicken (26%)
Rice (10%)	Dried chicken (25%)
Vegetables (7%)	Sweet potato
Natural ground bone	Peas
Seaweed meal	Potato
	Pea protein
	Alfalfa
	Chicken fat (3.1%)

Check the carb content – As we saw in the last chapter, too many refined carbohydrates wreak havoc on the gut, pancreas and your dog's insulin levels. I would avoid foods that have wheat soya and maize in them; look instead for sweet potato, oats, brown rice, carrots, etc.

Watch out for calories – Don't worry we're not getting into calorie counting here – just be aware that it's very easy to overfeed shop-bought food due to hidden calories. In wet food, elevated levels of protein and fat can drive up the calorie count. And in dry food, extra carbohydrate can make for high calorie counts that you could well do without. Refer to the table above for the ideal combination of food groups.

Note: food with high levels of protein and fat will tend to have proportionally lower carbohydrate content, which can be good for 'yeasty' dogs – i.e. dogs prone to itchy skin, paws and ears caused by Candida (a yeast overgrowth in the gut which thrives off starch).

Avoid:

- **Common, cheaper brands**: these contain heavily processed ingredients with too many amino acids, which put a strain on your dog's liver and kidneys
- **Food containing 'various sugars':** they're added to boost palatability
- **Antioxidants**: these are preservatives added to slow the rate at which oils and fats spoil and turn rancid; they include Ethoxyquin, BHA and BHT, which have been linked with tumour growth. Instead look for foods which use vitamin E (mixed tocopherols) and plant extracts (rosemary) as their preservative
- **'EC permitted colours':** these are added entirely for your benefit; the dog can't see them
- **Vegetable protein:** dogs digest meat protein better than vegetable protein, partly because the amino acid balance in meat is better suited to their gut

---

Embrace:

- **Meat meals**: a 'meal' is made up of animal parts, flesh, bones, blood and organ meat etc, which have been cooked and dehydrated to be reconstituted into pet food (more on this below). It doesn't sound particularly appetising, but believe me meat meals are a very good protein source
- **Chicken or poultry fat:** poultry (unlike the fat from red meat) when added in the right quantities, is an excellent fat source
- **Sugar beet pulp:** this is a great source of fibre, no added sugar

Commercial food myths

I love a good rumour, especially when it hangs about long enough to be elevated to mythical status and bandied about on pet food sites and forums... But enough is enough. Here are a couple of pet food myths I'd like to dispel:

Meat meal is sub-par meat

If you see the words 'chicken meal' rather than 'fresh chicken' on a label, it doesn't mean you are looking at an inferior food. Far from it. It's all about bioavailability. To explain, I need to tell you a chicken story.

When a chicken is dispatched at an abattoir, a vet will inspect the whole bird, including the pluck (heart, lungs, trachea, etc). Any sign of disease and it will be condemned, removed from the food chain and labelled a Category 1 animal by-product. Category 1 by-products are incinerated or sterilised and put into landfill.

All healthy carcasses are processed. The legs and breasts are removed, depending on what the supermarkets are calling for that week, and anything that's left (any meat, the carcass, head, feet, viscera, blood) is labelled Category 3 and it goes off to become meat meal.

The Category 3 offcuts are then put through a mincer; water is added and the lot is cooked at 110ºC for an hour. Then, fat is skimmed off the top and the mixture is dehydrated. What you end up with is a sort of 'cake', which is then ground down into fine flour, or meat meal. The fact that meat meal contains ground down bone makes it an extremely good pet food. This is because all the essential minerals found in bones – calcium carbonate, di-calcium phosphate and sodium – are rendered in an easily absorbable form and thus made more bioavailable to your dog.

So, claims that diseased meat or euthanised pets make their way into pet food are completely unfounded. I can't tell you how many times I've seen this myth spouted. As much as I criticise the dominant pet food companies for the nutritional quality of their products, no diseased meat or dead dog is making its way into the tins. You cannot fault the UK producers for their freshness and traceability.

Ash is bad
Although it is often interpreted as a waste by-product which has no business being in pet food, ash (sometimes also listed as crude ash, inorganic matter or incinerated residue) is in fact the technical term for mineral content. Ash is what's left behind after a proportion of the food has been incinerated to determine the mineral content. Along with protein, oil and fibre, it is the only other nutritional category that *must* be listed on a pet food label. An ash content of 6-9% is ideal.

Dry kibble has dental superpowers
I'm not sure how this rumour got started and gained enough traction to persist, but feeding dry food will not help keep your dog's teeth clean. Only regular brushing, and/or feeding a good seaweed supplement or raw meaty bones is ever going to give your dog that Hollywood smile. If dry, crunchy food did the trick, Oral B would be selling us digestive biscuits to be chewed diligently morning and night.

That's enough myths dispelled for one day.

How to read labels

While researching for this book I read a lot of pet food labels, and I mean a LOT. They don't make it half easy for you to choose the most nutritious and beneficial food for your dog. Once you get past the wackaging, words like natural, holistic and hypoallergenic, crop up like weeds.

For the record, 'hypoallergenic' means that a food is considered to be low allergen and shouldn't cause a reaction. 'Holistic' means very little in pet food terms, and 'natural' has a specific definition relating to additives (i.e. that the additives are natural, rather than synthetically produced). When we scan packets it is these words, helpfully added by Marketing Man, that we tend to notice.

We are all busy people who need to be able to understand what's in the dog food bag on the shelf, make a purchasing decision, hand over our hard-earned cash then get on with our day.

To that end, here's what you need to know when reading pet food labels. This definitive list acts as a recap for some of the topics we've touched on previously. First things first, ignore the hype on the front and turn straight to the back:

- Stay away from foods containing the five main causes of diet-related allergies: beef, wheat, dairy, soya and artificial colours and flavours

- Don't be fooled by price – expensive dog foods are not an always an indicator of quality
- Choose a food that lists ingredients singly – e.g chicken, rice, carrots – rather than as a group – e.g. meat and animal derivatives, cereals, vegetable protein
- Note the order of the ingredients. Meat or fish should always come first. Make sure they're not swiftly followed by two or more carbohydrate sources, such as rice, potato and maize, otherwise the total carbohydrate can account for more than the protein. Similarly, if ingredients such as fruit, vegetables, herbs and supplements occur further down the list than 'minerals', they will be in such negligible amounts that they are purely there for marketing purposes
- Avoid food that contains various sugars, which are only there for palatability and have no nutritional value
- Avoid anything listing EU permitted colours, artificial additives or flavours

The ultimate test when it comes to choosing a good commercial dog food is to ask yourself this: 'If I were to walk around the aisles of the supermarket right now, would I be able to buy the items in this list of ingredients as stand-alone products, more or less?' If the answer is yes – chicken, rice, carrots, peas, ground bone – it's more than likely a great dog food. If the answer is no – meat and animal derivatives, derivatives of vegetable origin, cereals and hydrolysed animal proteins – back on the shelf!

Raw food (commercial and 'DIY')

Pros:
- It's unprocessed
- Good for healthy teeth and gums
- Now available commercially as a complete dog food
- Feeding raw clears up a lot of health niggles
- Can reduce that doggy smell we all know and love

Cons:
- Raw food will need supplementing if you're doing it yourself

- It's crucial to get the meat/offal/fruit/veg ratio right
- Extra freezer space is required – the bigger the dog the more space you need
- Raw food requires safe handling as with any raw meat around the kitchen
- Bones can be a real hazard if you don't know what you're doing

If one type of feeding is going to divide opinion, it's serving up raw food. It is a real bone of contention (sorry!). It doesn't divide opinion along party lines either. Some vets love it because they see bouncy, healthy dogs with beautiful pearly white teeth; others think it's incredibly dangerous because they've spent time operating to remove splintered bones from a dog's gut. If it fits in with your lifestyle, your dog may thrive on it, but don't feel guilty for not feeding raw, which I know some of you do.

Feeding raw can have enormous benefits. For starters, you have less 'output' to clear up. Digestion improves, energy levels and weight seem to even out, your dog's skin, coat, eyes and teeth gleam. I'm not quite sure why this is or why all the raw-fed dogs I've ever met are a healthy weight, but in my experience that's definitely the case. I suspect it's down to the research that owners have put in to make it work, in turn becoming more attuned to their dog's needs.

Commercial raw food

In feeding raw you have two options, commercial raw food and 'DIY' raw food. As mentioned in the 'cons' list above, getting the balance of vitamins and minerals right is crucial, and the main benefit of commercial raw food is that it's made as a complete dog food so everything they need nutrition-wise will already be included.

If you're new to feeding raw, I suggest trying your dog on a commercial raw food first. Brands like Natural Instinct, Natures Menu and Nutriment are very good and are available online or from your local pet shop's freezer. As a guide, the ingredients in shop-bought raw food should resemble those in the table below. Add in the odd frozen raw treat as well: duck necks, bull pizzles and tripe sticks. Yum!

Commercial raw food
British chicken with bone (75%)
British chicken liver (5%)
Peas
Carrots
Butternut squash
Curly kale
Broccoli
Flaxseed oil
Sea kelp
Wheatgrass
Barley grass
Spirulina
Thyme, Bilberry, Brewer's yeast

Case study – Anita

George is my assistance dog, trained through Dog Aid Assistance in Disability. He is six years old.

When he was two and in training, his skin became very sore and itchy and started to erupt into weeping wounds. The itching drove him mad, he would scratch at his ears until they bled. Warm temperatures in particular were unbearable. In winter, he would have to go outside to cool his skin and as an assistance dog constantly in and out of shops, hospitals, etc, this was not very practical. He wasn't able to do his work. He was a very sad and unhappy dog.

After allergy tests, George was put on a raw food diet. This meant I was in complete control of what he was eating. It isn't an understatement to say raw food changed his life, and mine. Within three months his skin started to change, and now it's completely normal.

George now works as a full assistance dog. This means he is able to perform a whole host of tasks for me. Above and beyond the help, he is a loving companion. Is it too clichéd to say he's my best friend, because he really is. It's horrible to think I could have lost him.

'DIY' raw food

If you're going down the DIY route, the basic rule of thumb for making up your own meals is to feed either:

- ⅓ raw meat and bone, ⅓ cooked carbohydrates and ⅓ fruit and veg

Or if you are trying to avoid carbs*:

- 80% meat and bone, and 20% fruit and veg

*There is no need to eliminate carbohydrate from your dog's diet unless it's for health reasons, or your dog just does better without. Stick to the good carbs in the recipes below. You will soon find out what your dog does best on.

Here are a few things to remember when serving up raw food:

Practise good food hygiene
If you're using frozen raw meat, you must thaw it, make dinner with it, then feed it. Don't refreeze raw meat which was previously frozen, whatever you do. It's a misconception that dogs can eat food that's going bad

because they have strong stomach acid. Same as us, they don't want spoiled meat or fish, offal which smells off or old fruit and vegetables. Cooked rice that has been sitting around for a few days can be lethal. Besides, old food won't have the same nutritional value it did when it was fresh. Treat all the food you feed your dog with the same respect you would your own.

Blend/blitz starchy fruit and veg

The key to feeding your dog fruit and veg is to blend! blend! blend! Dogs don't eat in the same way we do; they barely chew. This is because digestion doesn't start in the mouth for them, it starts in the stomach. So when it comes to fruit and veg, they need a little help. The simplest way to do this is to blitz the food in either a food processor or with a hand blender. Basically this amounts to doing all the chewing for them so that the nutrition becomes available and is better absorbed. This applies if you are feeding raw or cooking your veg. My hand blender gave up the ghost recently, after 12 years of sterling service. Its replacement came with a mini food processor with a blade attachment. It holds about a litre and makes short shrift of a carrot.

Mix cooked veg with raw meat

Starchier vegetables like carrots, swede, turnips, for

example, become easier to digest when cooked. It won't mess up your dog's digestion to mix cooked veg and raw meat together, in fact it will put less strain on him as his gut is not trying to break down starchy matter.

This is one of those contentious areas where purists might object to the idea of feeding mixed cooked and raw, alluding to what would have been natural for 'dogs in the wild'. What I would say is this: think of what the vegetable matter in the gut of whichever wild animal the dog was eating had been through before the dog happened upon it. It wasn't cooked, granted, but it would have been pretty marmalised by the animal's acid and digestive enzymes – processed using a natural blender if you will.

Vary protein sources

Balance is important when raw feeding. When you are starting out and your dog is getting used to it, it's ok to feed a single protein, but after a couple of weeks you can start to chop and change. Lamb, pork, chicken, game and fish contain different levels of essential vitamins and minerals, all of which your dog needs. As an example: tuna contains three times the selenium of chicken or turkey. Selenium regulates the thyroid, mops up free radicals in the body and improves skin and coat condition. Lamb is high in zinc which is good for a healthy heart, and chicken is rich in vitamin B6 which boosts the immune system. It's up to you whether you stick to one protein per meal or a combination of meat and fish, or a combination of meats; choose whichever works best for you and your dog.

Make your own mince

Mince is a relatively cheap meat but it can be fairly fatty, especially lamb mince. Unfortunately lean lamb mince isn't as readily available as lean beef mince, so the best way around that is to mince or grind meat yourself. Chat to your butcher, shop at Lidl, Morrisons, Aldi and buy whole meat cuts (e.g. chicken legs and thighs – cut out the bone; pork cheeks, beef shin – all the cheaper cuts; lamb shoulder) and cut the big pieces of fat off. Ox cheek is also a good one. (Note: I say to avoid beef as it's often not well tolerated, but you can try it in home-cooked recipes. You'll soon know if it disagrees.) Then chop them up and whizz together in a food processor, or use the mincer attachment if you have one (you lucky thing). Whole cuts will probably be more expensive than buying a pack of mince, but you will get far more usable meat out of them. Don't be afraid of chopping up unusual cuts too, such as cow or pig cheeks. They are much cheaper and highly nutritious.

Don't be afraid of offal

Offal is the collective noun for the internal organs of an animal, aside from the muscle and bone. Heart, liver and kidneys are commonly available types of offal; tripe, intestines, brains, trotters, lungs and heads less so. They're all edible and most dogs love them.

When feeding raw, 20% of the meat and bone ratio (see p.66 above) can be made up of offal. Do be careful not to overfeed liver, however. I would stick to no more than 5% liver in the offal you are feeding. By its very nature, the liver mops up and stores vitamins and minerals, which can't be excreted by the kidneys. One such vitamin is Vitamin A, and if consumed in large quantities, it can cause joint pain and swelling, hair loss and cracked skin. So keep liver consumption down to a minimum, there's plenty more to choose from – who doesn't love a trotter! See my top offal recipe in the next chapter, which has the correct amount of liver measured out for you.

Bring back green tripe!

Green tripe deserves a culinary high five also. It's the unwashed stomach lining of a ruminant, a grazing animal: cow, sheep or deer. The white tripe you see in the butcher has been washed, fit for humans, but I will never understand why you can't buy green tripe at the butcher's for the dog. Green tripe is still full of enzymes that the animal's gut flora created as it digested its food. So it's very healthy for your dog and often a hit with fussy eaters. It isn't the most pleasant-smelling of ingredients (it stinks), but you can buy it minced and frozen in blocks from your local pet shop, which takes some of the stench out of it.

Feed bone

Raw bones can be fed a couple of times a week. They MUST always be raw, NEVER cooked. I'm amazed at how often people get this wrong. Cooked bones are harder, more brittle and will splinter easily. Raw bones are much softer, full of nutrition; and bones with a lot of meat on them are a meal in themselves.

Try:
- Chicken wings, drumsticks and carcasses
- Lamb shoulder, necks or leg bones
- Duck necks
- The smaller beef bones
- Pork ribs
- Whole heads

Most of these can be bought frozen in good pet shops but I tend to buy my chicken at the supermarket. If you don't feel comfortable feeding whole bones to your dog, then don't. There are alternatives. Rather than add a bone supplement, I would add commercial raw food which contains bone to your DIY raw feeding plan. Meat mixed with ground bone intended for pets will be safe. I wouldn't wing it and add ground bone yourself. It is often sold as fertiliser and it's hard to know what temperature it was heated to or for how long, both of which will affect its nutritional value.

Supplements you can add to a raw meal

If you opt for DIY raw feeding you're going to have a hard time getting all the vitamins and minerals your dog needs in a meal. It's nigh on impossible in fact. Granted, variety will go a long way to correcting any imbalance but you're going to have to add good supplements in there to get the range of essential fatty acids, calcium, phosphorus, sodium, and B vitamins they need. The list below offers a good basic guide:

- Fish oils
- Flaxseed oil
- Kelp or seaweed
- Brewer's yeast
- Extra-virgin coconut oil
- Raw apple cider vinegar

How to make the switch easy peasy

Whether you're going for the commercial or DIY option, the key to changing your dog to raw food (or to any new diet for that matter) is patience and a positive attitude. The older the dog, the more entrenched she is with her current diet, and the longer it may take to make the change.

You can switch from kibble to raw feeding overnight if you like. But if you want to move your dog over gradually – which I recommend, especially for older dogs – it's best to feed both raw and his current kibble for a while, but serve them separately. This is so that your dog gets used to the new texture of raw food. I recommend switching over seven days or so, gradually lessening the amount of kibble while increasing the raw food.

Here are a few tips and tricks you can employ to ease the transition:

Act natural – Dogs can sense stress in their owner at a hundred paces. So stay positive, act casual and try not to hover over them to see if they've taken to their new food.

Take your time – You don't have to rush this. It's a marathon, not a sprint; you're making a change for the rest of their lives. So chill. Leave your dog to get used to the new food. Doesn't matter if it takes all day.

One protein at a time – If you've been feeding your dog cooked chicken (or chicken-based shop-bought food), move him on to fresh chicken. If it's been lamb, move over to that. This way you're not hitting him with new flavours as well as textures all in one go. You can introduce new proteins slowly over time. Added bonus: it's a good way of spotting food intolerances.

Start with meat only, no bone – You can introduce bone after a week or so.

Introduce offal slowly – When your dog has been eating raw for a couple of weeks, introduce offal in tiny amounts. Most dogs tolerate heart, kidney and liver very well, but on the off chance that they don't, start slow and small.

That's pretty much it for raw feeding. Once you've got your dog going on raw, feel free to mix it up as much as you like (the meal plan in Chapter 5 is a good guide). The key is to get the nutritional balance right and make sure your dog isn't missing out on any vital vitamins and minerals. If there is a food your dog really doesn't like, add a good corresponding food supplement to compensate. There are bags of feeding plans, recipes and advice forums out there online. You'll be fine!

Case study – Maureen

I switched to raw feeding about 15 years ago. I breed Rottweilers and we were losing them very early with cancer and I think that was mainly down to the preservatives in their food. Anything past the age of seven was a bonus.Now, three generations later, we are getting them to 12 and 13, and have just lost one at 14, so I really advocate raw feeding.

I remember my vet calling to ask if he had upset me in any way because I was one of his top fee-paying clients once upon a time... If only he would recommend raw feeding to the other top fee payers, their dogs might be as healthy as ours. On average, I'd say 70% of my puppy buyers stick to raw feeding when they get their dog home – that is, unless their vets have anything to do with it!

Home-cooked food

Pros:
- If you're a savvy shopper, it's cheaper than buying dog food
- You know precisely what ingredients are going into your dog's dinner
- The recipes can be far more varied
- Your dog will take a warm home-cooked meal over a bowl of dog food any day
- It can clear up health problems caused by feeding poor-quality shop bought food

Cons:

- Time-consuming unless you cook in batches
- It can be hard to get the nutritional balance right
- Dogs can't eat everything we eat
- It can be expensive while you get your head around it
- If you're making it in bulk, storage can be an issue

There are many reasons why you might want to cook your dog's meals from scratch. Above and beyond having a calmer, happier dog, a distinct advantage is being able to select ingredients your dog likes, while avoiding those which set off problems. On top of that, you are feeding more nutrient-dense food, so your dog will need less of it. If you know where to shop and how to utilise food that would normally be resigned to the compost heap, it can be much more cost-effective than buying top-of-the-range dog food.

According to research, the average dog owner doesn't want to pay more than 50p a day to feed their dog. Fifty pence on the single most important thing we ever give to our dog? No judgement here, but if you feed your dog supermarket own-brands every week then you are probably part of that group. Hand on heart when I say this: feeding a dog at that price point just isn't viable today. As

I've said before, you are investing now to save money on vet bills later. And I can assure you that if you spend that little bit extra and home-cook, you can tick all the nutritional boxes.

In the recipe section coming next, I've costed all my recipes to an average of about 75p per meal (see p.78 for more details). To economise, I suggest preparing home-cooked recipes in batches, bagging the food up in meal-sized portions and freezing it. Great to have as back up if you run out of conventional food, too.

As with the DIY raw feeding method, one challenge of home-cooking is getting the nutritional balance right. You will definitely need to vary the ingredients you use to achieve this. Dogs require many of the same elements and minerals that we do – iron, copper, manganese, zinc, etc – but a good balanced diet will sort this out, see thedogdiet.co.uk for lots more information.

Overall, home-cooking can make a massive difference to your dog's health, especially if you're switching over from shop-bought food. A few years ago I was working on a TV programme about food additives in human food, and one of the things we wanted to find out was whether ready-meals were as nutritious as homemade dishes. We made a shepherd's pie from scratch. Then I took a middle-of-the-road ready-meal shepherd's pie from each of the big supermarkets and sent the lot off to a well-known food research establishment to be blind tested for their nutritional value.

My 75p promise

Just in case you don't believe me, and just to prove my point that it will not cost you loads of extra money to feed home-cooked, here is a break-down of my Boneless Burgers recipe:

600g mince
200g tinned fish
2 × raw eggs
200g vegetables

Total £3.89 to make a 1kg batch. That works out at 77p for 200g. If you compare that to a leading dog food, e.g. a Royal Canin adult 15kg bag at £56.99, a 200g serving comes out at 76p. And that's not super-premium food. Orijen works out at £1.29 for 200g.

You must do what works for you, according to what you can afford, and what you can fit into your life in a manageable way.

So go experiment and adapt as you will. After a couple of weeks you should really hit your stride; once you've had the thumbs up from the dog and chucked out that three-year-old bag of frozen spinach and discovered a bit of spare cupboard space, you'll be off like a rocket.

All the meals were measured for protein, fat, carbohydrate, salt and sugar levels. The ingredients listed on the ready-meal packets weren't as poor as we might have expected, but in comparison to the homemade version they were unimpressive. The homemade version had better protein levels, the lowest sugar and salt levels and wasn't bad in the fat stakes either.

The second part of the programme involved enlisting the help of a family of six who were asked to live additive-free for six weeks. Basically, if there was an additive in it, they couldn't eat it. This pretty much ruled out any processed food: no biscuits, fruit drinks, ready-meals or bread. Meat, fish, fruit, veg and rice were all fine but nothing could be added. Just imagine, not a whiff of a bacon sandwich for six whole weeks. Tragic.

Before the experiment started, we tested all the participants for cholesterol, blood sugar, vitamin and mineral levels. Six weeks later, we took bloods again: the results were staggering. Cholesterol and blood sugar levels were all down. Vitamin and mineral levels all up substantially, especially vitamin C. They had more energy, had lost weight, didn't suffer from that notorious 'afternoon dip', and were sleeping better. That's why I cook for my dog.

Where to shop and what to buy

While you would be totally within your rights to argue

that quality is costly, I'd have to disagree. When you think that the chicken which goes into pet food (Category 3) is made up of odds and ends from the same chicken you buy in the supermarket, you're not obliged to buy organic, free-range loveliness. Get your bog standard meat or fish from any supermarket you like. You will save money by looking out for unusual cuts or going shopping when it's likely to be marked down. Personally I like Lidl and Morrisons because all their meat is British and not outrageously priced. Morrisons do some odd cuts too which can be really good value.

Make friends with your local butcher and fishmonger. They do exist and are more than happy to help. If you're buying food for yourself there is often a cheeky bone or bag of offal to be had for pennies. Just repeat the Dog Diet mantra to yourself: I am choosing to spend money on good food now to save on vet bills later on.

How to do it

I recommend cooking in batches, which is cost-effective and means you almost always have something in the freezer for a lazy day. Say I've just cooked Nikita a chicken dinner, I put some in the fridge for the week, portion the rest up and freeze it. At the supermarket, I'm always on the look-out for bargains. If I don't need it there and then, I'll freeze it to cook up later. I make up different recipes one batch at a time so that I can vary what comes out of the freezer. It might be lamb mince with fresh vegetables and rice in one batch, followed by poached chicken, sweet potato and vegetables in another, or fish and vegetables in the next. You get the idea. Once I've got a batch of a few different recipes in the freezer I can vary what I feed every day. Add fruit, a *little* cottage cheese, peanut butter in a Kong as a treat and you're packing in the variety (more on treats later). A raw egg once in a while won't hurt, and if you're comfortable with it a fresh raw bone with a bit of meat on always goes down well.

When I think about BB, our rescue Bedlington, and how overweight she was when she arrived, I know this formula works. Nikita, too, is a stable weight now and her breath has greatly improved since I changed her over to home-cooked. She also loves eating raw food but that's a recent thing with her. Our dogs are energetic, but not crazy, and they're in great shape.

A word on supplements

If you add supplements to your dog's dinner, add them to the meal just before you serve it, not at the time of cooking. Most food supplements that I know of are to be given that way and can be delicate little things. Good oils for instance will lose any value if heated so are best kept in the fridge until you need them. There's a whole list of the different supplements and what they do after the recipe section.

The leftovers debate

To feed or not to feed your dog leftovers, that is the question. Some will say absolutely not; but if you're going to, keep to the really simple stuff and make them just an occasional treat. Don't give leftovers to the dog from the table; especially if she's a keen beggar, put them in her bowl instead. Nikita will beg at the drop of a hat and, being an ex-street dog, she's got that look nailed! No one is immune to her 'restaurant eyes'. She can even tear up if she's not getting her own way.

Leftovers the dog can eat:
- Meat – fat, skin and bones removed
- Fish – without bones
- Vegetables – cooked plainly without anything added
- Potatoes – if you've got a bit of mash left over, or a boiled potato – fine. Steer clear of anything Dauphinoise-like, or fried!

Leftovers the dog can't eat:
- Fatty meat or fatty foods – these can cause pancreatitis in dogs

- Foods with added salt and pepper – remove any seasoned skin from meat
- Stews and casseroles – fat, salt, red wine, Worcestershire sauce and onions are all bad for dogs
- Gravy – even homemade gravy will have salt or a salty stock cube in it, and if it's from a jar then best avoided: say no to Bisto!
- Fast food – no. Just no

Getting the balance right: the rule of thirds

Once you've got the hang of cooking for your dog and are confident enough to branch out on your own, you're aiming for ⅓ low-fat protein, ⅓ cooked carbohydrates and ⅓ vegetables and fruit in your recipes. If you're not feeding any carbohydrates at all, your dog is likely to be lethargic and prone to weight gain. Dogs, especially high-energy dogs on the go, need carbohydrate for energy. And complex, slow-release carbohydrates are good for her – sweet potato, quinoa, pearl barley, for example. What you need to avoid are the bad carbs as I mentioned previously – white rice, maize, wheat, and the carbs in kibble, which may have started out as complex, but have been rendered simple by the cooking process. These carbs give you a short burst of energy followed by a crash as the insulin kicks in. The recipes I recommend in the next chapter use complex carbs, which provide slow-release energy and keep your dog feeling fuller for longer. More importantly, they are great sources of vitamins and minerals.

Managing the change

How often have I heard the sentence, 'I tried to change his diet but the new food upset his tummy.' Of course it did. If you'd been eating the same thing, day in, day out for years, anything new would give you a little grief. But don't let that put you off; it's temporary, and in most cases a dog will adjust within a couple of weeks, if not sooner. Isn't it worth it for a healthier, happier dog? (Do you see what I did there, with the guilt?)

I've heard of owners offering their dogs different coloured foods (beef instead of chicken for instance) to tempt them. I'm afraid it won't make an iota of difference. We eat with our senses of sight and smell as well as taste, but dogs don't really get any value out of brightly coloured food because they don't see in the same way we do. Colours are muted for dogs, with more greys on their spectrum. Brightly coloured packaging and kibble is there purely for our benefit. If your dog could wander the supermarket aisles unhindered, a lack of colour wouldn't be a deal-breaker; she would probably head straight for the meat and fish counters rather than the pet food aisle.

Dog treats

Dog treats deserve their own section altogether. Here's why. When I started my website, *My Itchy Dog*, I was determined that the selection of dog treats I stocked should be the best you could get anywhere because research, experience and countless conversations have taught me that even if a dog's being fed the best food out there, chances are the treats she's getting will be nothing short of garbage! I don't know why we do it – maybe it's because we equate the treats we give our dogs to the treats we give ourselves.

What I mean is, I know that bag of Maltesers is full of sugar and fat, and I should probably only eat one or two instead of eating the whole bag (who does that?), but I scoff the lot regardless. When it comes to the dog, we're even less likely to be discerning. Especially if they've been eating healthy home-cooked meals all day... *Isn't that right, Susan? Who's a good girl?*

I've seen some of the worst examples of 'wackaging' on treats, and one myth that really gets my back up, already dispelled above, but worth re-iterating here, is the myth that crunchy treats will 'promote dental hygiene'. So, we all fall for the chocolate-wrapper-esque packaging and are taken in by grandiose health claims, while all the while gaining our dog's loving affection.

The good news about healthy dog treats is they don't

have to cost any more than the unhealthy versions. This is because they're usually made by smaller companies, who don't blow the budget on marketing, but concentrate on the ingredients. Again, forget the hype on the front and read the label.

As with other commercial food, look for treats with ingredients that are listed singly and not by categories, and you'll be fine. As an example, you can buy a bag of chicken-strip dog treats (ingredients: whole strips of real chicken – shocker, right?) made in the UK for £3.49, whereas a bag of 'dental' treats (ingredients: meat and animal derivatives, cereals, permitted colourants, etc) costs over £4.50 a bag. See: healthy treats don't cost a bomb.

One word of warning, I'd stay away from rawhide that's been treated, such as smoked rawhide or hide shoes with hide 'laces'. These are pretty efficient choke hazards in my view. All rawhide is washed and most is treated with preservatives, which don't have to be mentioned on the label. If your dog can't live without it, at least avoid flavoured rawhide – 'bacon' or 'cheese' rawhide should stay on the shelf. Try a deer antler – it won't make a mess and it lasts for ages – or a juicy bone from the butcher if you're not worried about the floor.

Don't forget you can always give your dog a simple, fresh treat, like a piece of carrot, broccoli or a slice of pear. These are cheap and healthy options and you're likely to have some lying around (look underneath that bag of

Maltesers). Let me say it again: human treats are not to be used as dog treats, people! By that I mean Rich Tea biscuits, toast and jam, Yorkshire pudding with gravy, and leftover pizza, all of which at one time or another customers have confessed they slip to the dog. Every night before bed, in the case of the toast!

To sum up...

So there we are: three different ways to feed your dog, all of them with their own pros and cons. Ultimately, of course, it's down to what works best for you and your dog but I hope it's become clear that giving your dog the same food day in, day out is a recipe for all-out boredom and long-term health problems.

I feed Nikita a combination of all three types – shop-bought/commercial, home-cooked and raw. She will eat anything except fish or any kind of cereal-based dog treat. (In her world if it looks like a dog biscuit, and it smells like a dog biscuit, it cannot be classed as food.) She won't eat dry kibble either unless it belongs to the cat and there is a power struggle in progress. I supplement her food with omega oils and a seaweed supplement.

In winter she and the cat are partial to a little scrambled egg and the occasional spoon of porridge – needless to say, no salt or sugar added. They are both in fine fettle, only a little paunch on Pearl, but she is 15 and some days she eats just to stop the dog from scoffing it.

Our much-loved and remembered lurcher, Bud, loved nothing more than a raw egg once in a while. He'd play with it, tease it along the patio floor, until he could bear it no longer, then crush it, eating the contents and shell, leaving nothing behind. I also have some lovely photos of him lying down next to a lump of cucumber. He liked to gaze at it for a while before demolishing that too.

Variety, balance, freshness and quality are the key to the continued health of my pets and hopefully yours.

Chapter 4

The recipes

Before I go into the recipes themselves, just a brief word on the tools of the trade. Whether you're preparing raw or home-cooked recipes for your dog, you don't need any fancy or expensive kitchen gadgets. In fact, you can't go far wrong with a pan and a potato masher. But there are some kitchen utensils which really are worth investing in if you don't have them already. I've listed them below in order of how frequently I use them (to make everyone's dinner):

- Hand blender – available from Argos for £4.49, but I particularly recommend the Cookworks £17.99 version which comes with a mini-whisk and chopper
- Large steamer – Prestige do a 3.8-litre three-tier steamer for £27.99; I've had mine for years, it's saved me lots of gas
- Sharp knife – inexpensive these days, doesn't have to be anything fancy

- Slow cooker – Tesco sell one for £14.99, which is great for making bone broth and casseroles
- A big plastic bowl for mixing ingredients

If any of these items is too expensive right now, put it on your Christmas or birthday wishlist, or check out freecycle.org. I got a spare freezer on there a couple of years ago!

Keep any plastic containers, from takeaways or ice cream, for instance; they're perfect for storing food in the freezer.

Home-cooked recipes

Proportions and measurements

I've laid out the recipes following our ⅓ protein, ⅓ carbohydrates and ⅓ fruit and veg principle. They're mostly in kilo measurements to encourage you to cook in bulk, store some in the fridge (use within two or three days) and build up a stash of variety in your freezer. If space is tight-to-non-existent, just reduce the measures to suit.

Ingredient weights in the recipes are there as a guide but don't stress about getting them spot on. If you're short of a carrot, substitute something else you have in which is safe for dogs (check against the table on p.37). This isn't Masterchef – there won't be any long pauses or steely-eyed stares, your dog won't be critiquing your command of flavour, and she's certainly not hanging out for a foam reduction! She will be much too busy stuffing her face.

I've said it before, but it's worth mentioning again; I don't add salt, pepper or use any gravy or stock cubes in my recipes because they are mostly salt themselves. Dogs have a phenomenal sense of taste without you adding 'depth of flavour', and salt is really bad for their kidneys.

A note on rice and barley

When a recipe calls for rice, I use brown or basmati in all my recipes. I choose basmati over long-grain because it releases energy more slowly and is healthier for your dog. For barley, I recommend whole-grain or brown barley over pearl barley if possible because it hasn't had the bran 'polished away' which means it's packed full of fibre and minerals. I don't use pasta in recipes ever; rice is far less likely to cause an adverse reaction than wheat and, as I said before, it releases energy slowly.

For the recipes that follow I use the cooked weight of rice or barley as an indicator of how much to include. This is so that you can either use leftover rice or, when you cook for everyone, know how much to siphon off for the dog. But generally speaking, the uncooked-to-cooked weight-ratio is 1:3; so 100g of uncooked rice will yield approximately 300g once cooked. This ratio is an approximation and depends on which brand of rice you use and how you cook it. Always cook to the packet instructions and make sure it's cooked right through. As we've seen, raw starch is one sure way to give your dog gut problems.

To peel or not to peel?

Much of the goodness in vegetables resides in the skin, so

when possible I would suggest you scrub rather than peel any veg in the recipes below.

Case study – Diane

Oscar suffered from bouts of tummy upsets when we first brought him home aged seven weeks. He did not seem to want to eat and as he was so underweight we worried that we might lose him. When he did eat he would have terrible diarrhoea and consequently was not thriving. He was miserable and had little energy.

Our vet established that he was allergic to most foods, including beef, chicken, lamb and duck. We started to buy more unusual meats to feed him, such as venison and rabbit. He would eat a little of the rabbit which I casseroled for him, but not every day, and he would not even touch treats. He would hide as soon as I started cooking his food and cower and shake.

Oscar was now almost three years old and weighed only 8kg. As a rather tall Border Collie this was underweight. Eventually, a specialist discovered he was producing a lot of helicobacter pylori bacteria in his gut which causes stomach ulcers in humans. The specialist believed that it was this overproduction of bacteria that was making Oscar feel sick and stifling his appetite.

The vet prescribed some anti-sickness drugs, which worked but we did not want him to be on these strong drugs all his life and so started to think about home-cooking. After some experimentation, we now have what we think is a winning formula. I still casserole fresh rabbit everyday but I top it with mashed potatoes, sweet potatoes and a selection of steamed veg such as peas or broccoli.

I make up a little of CSJ Gravy Works with the casseroled rabbit juice and pour it over, also including a Lintbells Yumpro Bio-Activ tablet. I sometimes have to tempt him to the bowl with a little apple or pear but as soon as he starts eating he really tucks in. I think that years of being afraid of food means he has developed a bit of a phobia. Once he starts to eat, you can really see that he is enjoying his food and, unbelievably, he does not leave anything now.

Our life was ruled by Oscar's non-eating but now we are relaxed. Aged four, he weighs 12kg and has much more energy. It is great to see him running around and enjoying life.

Simple Lamb Dinner (gluten-free)

This dinner is so simple I had to put it in the recipe name. Cook. Mix. Cool. Serve.

You can use any cut of lamb for this recipe, though mince will be the cheapest. Do chat to the butcher (he won't bite), and he'll be able to advise you on cheaper cuts and get them in for you. Lamb is a high-fat protein so cut as much of the fat off as possible before cooking. If using mince, cook it separately then drain most of the juice off while it's still hot; the fat will drain off too.

Ingredients

1kg lamb mince

1kg frozen mixed basic vegetables (nowt fancy – carrots, beans, peas and corn are just fine)

1kg cooked brown or basmati rice

Method

In a large heavy-bottomed pan cook the lamb (or other cuts) on a medium heat until it's thoroughly cooked through, drain off any fat. At the same time, cook the frozen veg in a pan large enough to fit your hand blender without redecorating the kitchen with bits of green bean in the process! Once the veg is cooked, drain off the water but leave enough in the pan to blend it into a loose porridge consistency. Using that hand blender (or a food processor), blend the vegetables together, then mix with the mince and add the cooked rice. Make sure they all coat each other well so any picky eaters can't find a pea worth spitting out.

Fancy Chicken Dinner (gluten-free)

One for when you have more time on your hands.

Ingredients
1½kg chicken thighs and drumsticks*
500g sweet potato
500g swede
250g cabbage any kind
250g broccoli, stalks and all
250g cauliflower, stalks too
250g green beans

> *I usually buy 2 x 1kg thigh and drumstick trays, use 1½kg for roasting (equating to roughly 1kg of cooked meat), and retain the other ½kg to feed to the dog raw another time.

Method
Roast the chicken pieces in one dish. Chop up the sweet potato (don't bother peeling it first) and bake with a little olive oil in another roasting dish (this is to prevent the

sweet potato absorbing all the chicken fat).

While the meat and sweet potato are roasting, chop up all the other veg. Add the chopped swede to cold water in the bottom section of your steamer (or regular pan) and cook until soft. While that's cooking, steam the rest of the veg in batches in the top two tiers. It's important to cook each type of veg separately as they cook at different rates. You can do this in separate pans but you will save a fortune in electricity or gas if you can get hold of a tiered steamer.

Once the chicken is cooked, remove from the roasting dish leaving the fat behind, and set aside to cool. The sweet potato shouldn't have any fat, so just leave it to cool. When you can strip the chicken without burning your fingers, remove the meat from the bones, bin the skin and either save the bones for broth or put them in the bin too. Don't ever give cooked bones to a dog.

Drain off most of the water from the cooked swede, but leave a little behind in the pan for moisture. Add the roasted sweet potato to the swede water and blend together with your hand blender. A few handfuls at a time, tip the rest of the veg into the swede and sweet potato mixture until it's all mashed together. If your pan isn't big enough, you may want to split it into two batches or do the lot in a food processor if you have one.

Chop up the roast chicken meat into very small pieces and mix that into your potato and vegetable mash.

Voila!

If you've had enough of cooking by the time you've made this recipe for your dog, just syphon off some for yourself. Add a little butter and season well. Sorted. Much healthier than ordering a takeaway!

Beef Balls

A great recipe when you're worried about portion control – you hardly have to think about it!

Ingredients
1kg beef mince (no more than 10% fat)
1kg packet of frozen basic mixed vegetables
500g sweet potato
500ml bone broth (see recipe on p.130 below) or water
450g cooked whole-grain barley

Method
Brown the beef mince in a big heavy bottomed pan. Boil or steam the whole bag of mixed vegetables separately, then drain and add to the mince. Blend the lot together. Chop up the sweet potato (don't bother removing the skin), then add to the pot. Pour the bone broth or water over the mixture and stir well, bringing to the boil. Reduce to a simmer, cover with a tight-fitting lid and simmer until the everything is cooked through and most of the water is

absorbed. Add the cooked barley and blend together.

You should be left with a fairly solid mix. Let it cool, then weigh out a meal portion to suit your dog. (Remember your 15% reduction if you're trying to get weight off your dog. So, if you would normally feed your dog 200g, reduce your beef ball size to 170g.) Roll it into a ball and lay it on a sheet of greaseproof paper on a baking tray to harden. Serve up!

Freeze any leftovers. Because of their shape, they are very handy to bag up in meal-sized portions. Keep frozen for up to a month and take out of the freezer the night before you need them or feed it frozen on a hot day.

Beef, Offal and Potato Stew (gluten-free)

Meaty, unctuous loveliness. A great one served warm in winter. Not that I spoil my dog or anything…

Ingredients
800g stewing steak
75g heart
50g liver
75g kidney
A little vegetable oil for frying
500g carrots, unpeeled
250g broccoli stalks and all
250g frozen chopped spinach

1 clove garlic, chopped
500ml bone broth or water
800g cooked basmati rice or whole-grain barley
A handful of parsley, chopped

Method
Heat the oven to 170°C, 325°F or Gas 3. Cut the stewing steak and heart into small cubes. Slice the liver and kidney into smallish pieces but not so small they just become mush; they should retain form and shape. Add a little vegetable oil to a heavy bottomed pan and brown the meat and offal in batches. Retain any juices or liquid produced by the browning meat. Transfer the meat and any liquid into a casserole dish.

Chop the carrots and broccoli into small pieces. Add the chopped vegetables, spinach, chopped garlic and bone broth or water to the meat, give it a good stir, put on a tight lid (or cover it with foil if you're lidless) and put it in the oven. Cook for approx 1 hour or until the carrots are cooked right through. Keep an eye on the liquid levels and top up as necessary. Add the cooked rice (or barley), stir in the chopped parsley and serve.

Chicken and Vegetable Stew (gluten-free)

Dead easy to make, takes five minutes to put together.

Ingredients

1.5kg fresh chicken thighs and drumsticks
500g carrots, unpeeled, chopped
500g broccoli including the stalk, chopped, or a bag
 of frozen
500g cauliflower, chopped
250g spring greens, chopped
1 clove garlic, chopped
500ml bone broth or water
A glug of vegetable oil

Method

Mix the whole lot together in an oven-proof dish with
a lid, cover with broth or water and bake in the oven at
170ºC, 325ºF or Gas 3 until it's all cooked. Allow it to
cool, then pick the meat from the bones. Make sure you
trawl for any bones left behind, especially the really thin
ones, and throw them away, along with the chicken skin.
Give it a light mash to bind it all together and serve.

Skin & Bones

A hearty recipe for when you want to put some meat on
a skinny dog. Perhaps your dog has lost weight due to
illness, or you've just adopted a scrawny stray from the
rescue centre who needs food and a whole lot of love: this
is your answer.

Ingredients
Vegetable oil
750g minced beef, pork or lamb
250g mixed heart, neck, liver – no more than 50g
  of liver in total
1kg bag of frozen mixed vegetables
500ml bone broth or water
900g cooked rice or barley
2 large eggs, hardboiled and chopped
A large handful of parsley, chopped

Method
Heat up the vegetable oil in a large, heavy bottomed pan.
Brown the mince and giblets. Add the frozen veg, cover
with the water or spoon in the broth, put the lid on and
turn down to a simmer. Check the liquid level after a few
minutes and add more if it looks like the mixture is drying
out.

When there's only a bit of liquid left, it's done. Add
the cooked rice, the chopped hardboiled eggs and parsley,
give it a stir and serve.

Top tip: when serving as leftovers during the week,
add a good glug of omega oil right before your dog
digs in; I like Yumega Plus.

Fish Friday (gluten-free)

An easy-peasy fish recipe – basically fish pie for dogs.

Ingredients
500g bag frozen white fish fillets*
350g bag frozen salmon fillets
500g potatoes, chopped not peeled
500g frozen peas
250g spinach
250g broccoli, chopped
2 large eggs, hardboiled
A large handful of parsley, chopped

> *If you have time, defrost the fish beforehand; it
> will poach much more quickly this way

Method
Fill a deep pan with water, add the frozen fish fillets and
bring to a simmer. Cover and poach the fish slowly until
it's cooked all the way through. If you defrosted the fish
beforehand, just bring the water to a simmer, cover and
turn the heat off. It should be cooked through in ten
minutes or so. Chop the potatoes and boil in unsalted
water until soft. Mash them up without milk or butter.
No salt or pepper either. While the potatoes are boiling
(at the bottom of your steamer), steam the peas, spinach
and broccoli.

Once cooked, transfer the fish to a large bowl and leave to cool. Meanwhile, whizz all the vegetables together using a hand blender or food processor. Return to the fish and add the chopped egg and parsley. Mix until they bind together. Then add in the mashed potatoes, blended veg and mix again. Portion it up and serve.

The two recipes that follow are great for a day out or when you're travelling. Take a sandwich for yourself and serve up these great picnic snacks for your dog and doggy friends. They go well with the muffins you'll find in the treats section (yes, really!).

Salmon & Green Bean Fishcakes (gluten-free)

This is a clean and simple meal that's easily digestible (i.e. good for a dog who's recovering from illness). Dogs need protein and they also need fibre; this recipe does it all by including beans.

Ingredients
400g tin salmon
400g tin green beans
400g mashed potato, including skin (no butter, salt or milk added)
1 tbsp vegetable oil

Method

Drain the tin of salmon and flake it into a bowl. Empty the tin of green beans into a sieve and rinse under a cold tap. Chop the beans finely and mix together with the fish. Now add the mashed potato, and the oil and mix the lot together until it's all good and blended. Serve cold or warm it up. Any leftovers can be kept in the fridge for a couple of days.

Chicken Salad (gluten-free)

A good one for hot days, loaded with easily digestible protein.

Ingredients

1 chicken leg, roasted and left to cool
1 small tub of cottage cheese (full fat)
1 carrot, unpeeled, grated
A handful of green beans
A handful of parsley, chopped
A glug of good omega oil added just before eating
  (I like Yumega Plus)

Method

Pick the cold meat off the chicken leg and discard the skin and bones. Chop the meat up roughly, put it in a bowl and mix together with the cottage cheese. Add the grated carrot. Steam the green beans, run them under cold water, then chop and add to the mixture, along with the parsley and oil. Mix the lot together and serve.

Chicken Pupsicles (or Soup) (gluten-free)

When the weather starts to perk up, I make these in anticipation of the hot days ahead, and freeze them in ice cube trays. Because it's a blended recipe and you can't detect the veg, my cat is a fan too. Remember which are the chicken cubes and which are real ice; they do nothing for a gin and tonic!

Ingredients
1kg tray of fresh chicken thighs and drumsticks
1kg bag of frozen vegetables
500ml bone broth or water

Method
Put the chicken pieces and vegetables in a heavy-bottomed pan and just cover with broth or water. Bring to the boil, then turn down to a simmer for around 30 minutes, or until everything is cooked through. Turn off the heat and leave to cool. Take the meat off the bones and discard bones and skin. Then blend everything together – meat, veg and liquid – either in a food processor or with a hand blender. If the resulting mix is a little too thick, add some

cold water to thin it a little. Pour it into ice cube trays and freeze. Dole out a few cubes on a hot day to keep your dog cool and entertained. You can use a whole chicken for this recipe. I prefer pieces because they take a lot less time to cook through than a whole bird. This also works well as a warm soup in winter.

Christmas Dinner for Dogs

Did you know that if we wanted to walk off the average Christmas lunch we would have to march, non-stop, for 36 hours? Apparently. We really go to town on the high-fat, high-salt options on Christmas Day, making a human Christmas lunch thoroughly unsuitable for Tilly or any of her four-legged guests. This is an alternative (low fat, no salt) festive treat for your dog. Make it in advance to save yourself an extra job on the day.

Ingredients
A glug of vegetable oil
100g minced turkey
50g cooked rice
1 small carrot, unpeeled, grated
A couple of Brussels sprouts, finely chopped

Method
Heat the oil in a small frying pan. Add the mince and cook

through. Stir in the rice, grated carrot and sprouts. Put a lid on the pan and let it steam for a few minutes, allowing the rice to soak up the meat juices and the vegetables to soften. When it's all thoroughly cooked, remove from the heat and allow to cool right down before serving.

Love your leftovers!

For those of you who cook from scratch, there is a lot of food you throw away that will make an absolutely cracking addition to your dog's dinner. So while it's not entirely free because you paid for it in the first place, you're getting added bang for your buck by adding it to the dog's dinner. I've separated it into veg and non-veg.

Vegetables

Get yourself a plastic food container with a lid and use it to store any of the following in the fridge for a couple of days:

- Brussels sprouts, the outer leaves and the bottoms if you cut those off too
- Broccoli stalks and leaves
- Cauliflower centres
- The clean outer leaves of cabbages and kale
- Any green bean ends from topping and tailing

- Carrot peelings

Once you've got a little stash, either steam when cooking something else on the stove or, add a little water, cover and pop them in the microwave. Once they're cooked, use a hand blender and whizz the lot together. This yields a good veggie mash to mix in with cooked meat or fish.

My other top tip is: go blackberry hunting. They are everywhere, not just in the countryside, in towns and cities, too. I've got them out in the back alley behind my house. A handful is a great source of vitamin C.

Non-veg

- Raw bones – lamb shoulder or whole chicken carcass. Take the meat off the bones to use for whatever you're cooking, then simply give the raw bones to the dog. A lamb shoulder bone can occupy Nikita for a good hour as she picks off all the bits of meat. A chicken carcass does the same, plus she eats some of the bones too. I don't give her the whole carcass as that would be too much for a 9kg dog, but a bigger dog could eat the lot.
- Cooked bones (for broth) – fish, chicken, lamb, pork and beef – any from a leftover

roast, or raw bones will do. Put them in a slow cooker cover with water, squeeze the juice of a lemon into the mix and make a stock (see the bone broth recipe on p.130).
- Poultry giblets – if you ever get your mitts on poultry giblets of any kind, or know a friendly butcher who's giving them away, grab 'em! Great nutrition, can be fed cooked or raw.
- Fish skins – chop finely, cooked or raw, without bones and add them to food.

This is by no means an exhaustive list but you get the idea. Have a look at what you throw away. As long as it's fresh and safe for dogs to eat, then why not use to boost your dog's next meal?

Raw food recipes

As I've said, I believe in cooking starchier vegetables rather than serving them raw. So some of the recipes following have a mixture of raw meat and cooked veg.

Make Your Own Offal Mix

This is a hearty staple to have onhand to add to raw food recipes to provide extra nutrition. There are some pre-prepared offal mixes out there, but it's pretty simple to make your own. Especially if you want to keep a check on the amount of liver. I will specify which recipes below would benefit from an addition of offal mix, and how much of it to add.

This is a kilo mix you can make, portion up and freeze. You should be able to get all the off-cuts in the list below from your butcher and most from the supermarket, with the exception of tongue and tripe. These ingredients are just a guide; if you know your dog dislikes or is intolerant to one or another of them, just cut it out.

Ingredients
200g tongue
100g liver

250g heart
250g kidney
200g tripe

Method
Mix all the ingredients in a food processor or chop roughly. Then portion it up and either bag it or put into ice cube trays, and freeze. Make sure you get the liver mixed in well and spread evenly across the bags.

Stuffed Beef Pipes

Raw trachea, stuffed and frozen. Dinner of champions!

Ingredients
1 packet of 2 × Natural Instinct frozen beef pipes
200g raw broccoli, finely chopped
200g cooked and mashed sweet potato, unpeeled
200g raw mince of any meat you like

Method

Tip: Because you don't want to the pipes to defrost only to refreeze them, make the stuffing mixture first and let it cool. Then take the pipe out of the freezer, fill it up and get it back in the freezer within a few minutes so it doesn't get the chance to defrost.

Take a pipe, stand it upright in a glass or mug. Spoon in 50g of the raw broccoli and push it right to the bottom. Mix the sweet potato together with the mince then shove 200g of the mix into the pipe. Top it off with another 50g of broccoli.

Take it out of the mug and push both ends in to pack it all together. Then put it back in the freezer and freeze solid, or give to your dog straight away.

Turkey Dinner

Ingredients
1kg raw turkey mince
1kg raw and chopped mixed green leafy veg – spinach, kale, cabbage (even red cabbage – who cares if it's not green)
500g cooked and cooled whole-grain barley
500g cooked and cooled sweet potato, skin on

Method
Mix the raw turkey mince with the chopped green leafy veg (if you have a food processor, whizz the veg in that, for speed) add the cooked barley and sweet potato, mix and serve.

Beef Cheeks

This cut isn't often in demand, so it's a relatively cheap cut. I've seen this on a raw pet food website for just under £3 a kilo.

Ingredients
800g beef cheeks
250g mix of cooked root vegetables – carrots, turnips, swede, celeriac etc, unpeeled
250g raw broccoli, chopped
500g raw green leafy vegetables
200g offal mix
1kg mix of cooked rice and whole-grain barley

Method
Dice the beef cheeks, steam or boil the root vegetables; chop the raw broccoli and leafy vegetables, then add the offal mix, the rice and barley, and bind the lot together. Shape the mixture into balls in accordance with how many grams you are feeding your dog.

Fancy Eggs

A fun, healthy treat for a big dog or a whole meal for a small one.

Ingredients

1 egg, hard-boiled
1 tbsp of mince, chopped meat or fish (raw)

Method

Peel the hard-boiled egg and slice it in half lengthways. Remove the yolk and mash it together with the meat or fish. Spoon the mix equally in to the dip where the yolk was. Serve.

Boneless Burgers

Ingredients

600g raw mince – any meat combination you like
200g tinned fish in water – sardines, tuna, salmon
2 raw eggs, including the shell
200g vegetables – kale, parsley, broccoli, spinach, cucumber, cabbage (skin, outer leaves and peel on, chopped or diced in a food processor)

Method

This is a great one for the food processor or hand blender. Mix the mince and fish together in a bowl. In another bowl break the eggs, throw the shells in after them and add the chopped vegetables. Blend the veg and egg together until the shells are well crushed. Now mash the veggie-eggy mush in with the meat and fish.

If you're doing this in a food processor, the whole lot can go in and be blitzed together. Shape into patties. Gone in seconds!

Grain-Free Chicken Dinner

Ingredients
750g fresh boneless and skinless raw chicken
50g liver
50g kidney
100g cooked and cooled sweet potato, skin on
50g spinach, chopped
1 clove of garlic, chopped
1 tbsp organic coconut oil

Method
Roughly chop the chicken, liver and kidney. Roughly mash the cooked sweet potato with a fork and add that to the meat. Finally, add the spinach and garlic, and the coconut oil to the meat and potato mix.

Fishy Dinner

Ingredients
800g oily fish, whole or with heads removed
150g offal mix
1 raw egg, shell and all
1kg mixed veg and fruit – carrots, cabbage, broccoli,
  green beans, kale, spinach, any berries, apples and
  pears (no seeds, but outer leaves, skin/peel on)
1 clove garlic
1kg cooked rice or barley
1 tbsp organic coconut oil

Method
Chop the fish into largish lumps; add the offal mix and
raw egg and blitz together in a food processor. Stand well
back when you take the lid off, it's going to smell 'interesting'. Put the mix into a bowl big enough to contain all
the ingredients and set aside.

Blend the fruit and veg and garlic clove in the food
processor in batches, making sure it's well chopped and
thoroughly mixed. Put in the bowl with the fish, add the
cooked rice or barley and the coconut oil, and combine
the lot together.

Treats

There are some phenomenal dog treats on the market these days. But try and get them from your local pet shop or a reputable online store, as pretty much every treat on offer in a supermarket will be inferior, undoing all the hard work you're putting in to her food.

Having said that, I love a homemade treat. What makes them especially attractive is that they're perfect for dogs who are on a special diet. If your pooch is on a prescription food to help joints for instance and you don't want to tamper with what you're feeding, these treats can be used to break the monotony.

Meat and Lentil Muffins (gluten-free)

Ingredients
2 x 400g tins of cooked lentils, drained and rinsed
2 courgettes, skin on, roughly chopped
1 x 500g bag of frozen chopped spinach
1kg mince – lamb, chicken or pork

Method
Preheat the oven to 170ºC, 325ºF or Gas 3. Mix the lentils, courgettes and spinach with a hand blender or in

a food processor until you've got a good paste. Add to the mince and mix it all together with a wooden spoon (or by hand!). Now portion it up into small balls, rolling them into shape with your hands. Put them on a greased baking tray and bake for around 15 minutes. Serve them warm or store in an airtight container in the fridge or freezer. I pack a few frozen muffins into my backpack so they've defrosted when the dog gets them a few hours later.

Turkey, Pear and Oat Muffins (gluten-free)

Ingredients
2 large pears, skin on
1kg lean turkey mince
1 large courgette, skin on, finely chopped
125g porridge oats
2 large eggs (reserve the shells)
2 tbsps vegetable oil

Method
Preheat your oven to at 200ºC, 400ºF or Gas 6. Core your pears, chop them up and put them in a pan with 100ml water. Bring the mixture to the boil, then simmer until the pears are soft enough to mash with a fork. Don't add any sugar – there's enough in the fructose in the pears. You want to end up with a nice runny mix, so add more water if necessary.

Put the turkey mince, courgette, porridge oats, pear compote, eggs and vegetable oil in a large bowl and mix well. Wrap the eggshells in a tea towel, then take to them with a rolling pin and don't stop until they're a fine powder. Now tip them into the bowl too and mix everything together. Roll the mixture into balls – the size you settle on is for you and the dog to work out between you! Bake on a greased baking tray for 20 minutes. Turf out onto a wire rack, and allow to cool.

Veggie Seedy Patties

These are a wheat-free treat containing lots of good fibre. Quite calorie-dense, so definitely a treat and no more.

Ingredients
50g sunflower seeds
250g oat flour
1 tbsp ground flaxseed
5 tbsp olive oil
1 tsp fresh parsley, finely chopped
125ml water

Method
Preheat the oven to 180ºC, 350ºF or Gas 4. Chop up the sunflower seeds with a knife or stick them in the food processor. Put them in a bowl with the rest of the

ingredients and mix together until you've got a good dough. Break the dough off into pieces about the size of a gobstopper (about 20g per piece) and flatten each one down lightly with a fork. Put these rough patties on a greased baking tray and bake for 30-40 minutes. Cool on a wire rack. They can be stored in an airtight container or in the fridge for up to a week.

Jerky (gluten-free)

Jerky for humans and rawhide for pets is often treated with preservatives. Making your own is a good option if you've got the time and the inclination.

Ingredients
2 boneless and skinless chicken
2 large sweet potatoes, peeled

Method
Preheat the oven to 100ºC, 200ºF Gas 1. Remove any fat from the chicken, peel the sweet potato and slice them both into 5mm thick strips. Lie them on a lightly greased baking sheet (I use good greaseproof paper for this) and bake them for a couple of hours. The strips should be hard and dry, not soft.

The aim is to get as much moisture out of them as possible so they don't spoil. Leave them to cool on a wire rack, they should store for up to two weeks in the fridge in an air tight container.

Apple and Cheese Treats

I don't know any dog who doesn't like cheese, especially hard cheese. A good cheddar always goes down well, in very small amounts, of course. So try these out. The combination of the sweet apple and savoury cheese means they won't hang about for long.

Ingredients
150g apple, de-seeded, roughly chopped
400g oat flour
100g porridge oats
150g mature cheddar, grated
2 tbsp vegetable oil

Method
Preheat the oven to 180ºC, 350ºF or Gas 4. Chop up the apple, remove the core and cook it with a little water in a small pan. When it's nice and soft, set it aside to cool. Mix the stewed apple with all the other ingredients, then add enough water to bind the mixture together to form a dough (about 150ml). On a floured surface, roll the dough out to about 1cm thick and cut into biscuits – how big will depend on the size of dog they're intended for.

Lay them on a lined baking sheet and bake until they're golden brown. Turn off the oven and leave them to cool down, dry out a little more and harden. When the oven is cold, take the biscuits out and treat! Store any extras in an airtight container.

Liver Cake

By far and away the easiest, tastiest and most adored treat you can make for your dog. The downside is it does smell out the kitchen, so make it on a day when you can throw open all the doors and windows.

Ingredients
250g liver
125g oat flour
2 large eggs
2 cloves of garlic

Method
Preheat the oven to 180ºC, 350ºF or Gas 4. Line a greased cake tin or tray with greaseproof paper. Roughly chop the liver or whizz it with a food processor or hand blender. Add the flour, eggs and garlic to the liquidised liver and whizz a second time. Pour or shovel the mixture into your lined tray and put it in the oven to cook for 30 to 40 minutes. You'll know when it's cooked because the cake

should just bounce back a little when you prod the top with your finger. Take it out of the oven and leave to cool on a wire rack. When the cake is cold, remove it from the tin and cut into small squares. Portion it up into bags and freeze.

Tuna Cake

If liver is too rich for your dog, you can make a tuna cake instead. Drain a 250g can of tuna (tuna in oil works better in a food processor), blitz it in the blender or processor, then add the rest of the ingredients for the liver cake and repeat as above. Makes equally smelly, and therefore very good, training treats.

Birthday Cake

Well, I couldn't leave this section without adding a cake mix for special occasions. Use this recipe for special days. Makes enough for four dogs.

Ingredients
For the cake:
4 eggs
200g peanut butter (the kind with no salt, sugar or palm oil added)

50ml sunflower oil
50ml honey
2 medium carrots, unpeeled, grated
200g oat flour
1 tsp baking powder

For the icing:
3 tbsp Greek yoghurt
1½ tbsp peanut butter

Method
Preheat the oven to 180ºC, 350ºF or Gas 4. In a large bowl, combine the eggs, peanut butter, oil and honey, and mix well.

Stir in the grated carrot, then add the flour and baking powder and fold it into the mixture. Pour the cake batter into a greased and lined cake tin and bake for 40 minutes. Leave it to cool on a wire rack for a few minutes, before turning it out of the tin.

When it is completely cool, you can add the icing. Simply combine the Greek yoghurt and peanut butter, put the mixture into the fridge for 20 minutes to stiffen a little, then spread it on to the cake with a pallet knife.

Zero-Effort Dog Treats

Fresh, raw bones – If your dog likes a bone (and most dogs do), find a butcher who'll either save one or get one in for you. I buy mine by the tray, for a couple of quid, and freeze them. Nikita loves them straight out of the freezer, especially on a warm day. However, she isn't a dog who will bear down on a bone with the full might of her molars. She happily spends time picking the meat off with her front teeth. If your dog likes to devour a bone right off the bat, I wouldn't give them a frozen one in case it shatters. If Nikita were that way inclined I would only ever give her bones from the fridge or at room temperature. Bones MUST be raw, as cooked bones splinter and are very dangerous for dogs. Go for bones that are larger than your dog's mouth, preferably with a little marrow. She's then occupied for ages, scraping the marrow out, picking off bits of meat left on the bone, and allowing you to get on with your own stuff. If your dog is eating a bone in the garden, I'd either bring it in at night or discard it after she's done with it. That way you're not attracting foxes into the garden or parasites and flies on to the bone for your dog to revisit later.

A free-range egg, shell and all – No dog treat is easier to get your mitts on at short notice, or better for the dog. An egg, in its shell (maybe crack it just a little so your dog knows there's something worth working towards inside) once or twice a month, preferably outside(!), will do wonders for his skin and coat, brain and heart. An egg is a complete food, full of amino acids, vitamins A, B2, B6 and B12, iron, calcium, potassium and on and on. It is also one of the few foods in the world that naturally contains vitamin D.

Fruit – Berries of all types, fresh or frozen, contain all sorts of good antioxidants. A slice of cold watermelon – seeds removed – is a hit with some dogs.

Smoothies

Another good stand-by if you have a picky dog or a skinny one you're trying to fatten up. They're also very good frozen as treats to help your dog cool down on a hot day.

There's no hard and fast rule here – just keep the ingredients simple and few. Use whatever fruit or veg you have to hand as long as it's on the safe-for-dogs list. Use goat's milk rather than cow's milk, or water, for liquid. Stick it all in a blender and whizz! All gluten-free.

Banana fruit smoothie
½ banana
A handful of blueberries
100ml Toplife goats' milk for dogs

Peanut butter smoothie
For a luxury treat and only a little, as this one is pretty high in calories

½ banana
1 tsp flaxseed
1 tsp peanut butter
Toplife goats' milk for dogs

Apple and Carrot Smoothie

1 apple, skin on, seeds removed
1 carrot, unpeeled
Water to blend

Vitamin B Special

A handful of kale
1 pear, skin on, seeds removed
1 tsp coconut oil
Water to blend

Healing recipes

Bone Broth

This is a stock really full of vitamins and minerals and low in fat and salt. I make a batch whenever we have a roast or I can get hold of a bag of bones from the butcher. Bag it up or stick it in ice cube trays and freeze. Pour over food, serve on its own warm or cold (never hot), or use it in most of the recipes here requiring liquid.

This broth is an effective and incredibly cheap way of getting a lot of nutrition into your dog or cat in an easily digestible form. I use chicken in this example but you can use beef, lamb, game and pork bones. Use it as a way of:

Keeping joints supple and pain free – Meat carcasses are full of glucosamine, chondroitin, hyaluronic acid and lots of collagen. These nutrients are transferred into the broth and your dog absorbs them to use in their own joints, cartilage and ligaments. A free, bioavailable joint supplement if you will, without additives.

Detoxing your dog – Broth contains glycine, a simple amino acid that is great for detoxing the liver and kidneys.

Healing a leaky gut – Our guts are lined with miniscule holes, which allow the nutrients from the food you eat to pass from the intestines into the body. A diet which is high in poor carbohydrates and stress are just two reasons these holes can increase in size. Bigger holes means things that shouldn't pass into the body do. This causes an inflammatory response known as leaky gut. Symptoms of a leaky gut can be wind, diarrhoea, fatigue, aching joints and food allergies. The gelatine in the broth blocks or narrows these holes. The aforementioned glycine also soothes an inflamed gut. Just so you know.

Giving medicine – I guarantee this broth is irresistible to all dogs. It's deeply savoury and will entice any picky eaters on long or short-term medication, or supplements.

Ingredients

A whole uncooked medium chicken or a fresh chicken carcass, or one left over from a roast, skin removed
Water to cover
Juice of one lemon or 2 tbsp apple cider vinegar – whatever you have to hand. (The citric acid encourages the bones, ligaments and tendons to hand over their nutritious treasures.)

Method

If you're using a whole chicken, place it in a cast-iron lidded pot, cover with water and bring to the boil. Simmer for a few minutes until any scum has surfaced, and remove. Then transfer everything into a covered slow cooker. Simmer for 4 hours, then remove the chicken and turn the slow cooker down to low. Put the lid back on and let the juices continue cooking. When the chicken is cool enough, remove all the skin and meat. Reserve the meat for the dog or cat, especially if they're not well because this will be very digestible by now. Return the carcass to the pot.

If you're using a chicken carcass left over from a roast, this is your starting point. Make sure to discard any part of the carcass you've seasoned with salt and pepper first, especially the skin. Put it in a slow cooker and cover with water, as above.

Add the lemon juice or apple cider vinegar, put the lid back on and leave it to cook for at least 24 hours. The longer you leave it (max 48 hours, and make sure it's on low and you keep an eye on it), the more goodness is drawn from the bones, tendons and ligaments into the liquid. I do mine at the weekend when I can keep an eye on it. When it's done, discard the large bones and strain the liquid to remove any tiny bones which may be hiding. (Another option is to liquidise the broth just to be sure.) Allow to cool. Remove any fat from the surface and chuck that in the bin.

You should be left with a gloopy, gelatinous pot of gold which smells more like chicken than any chicken you've ever come across in your entire life. This broth is delicious and full of highly available and digestible nutrition. Syphon some off for your own chicken soup base, keep some in the fridge for use over the next few days and freeze the rest.

Anti-Inflammatory Oat Treats

These beauties come courtesy of Eloise Walduck, who makes them for her greyhound. A great dog treat containing ingredients which have anti-inflammatory effects on the body.

Ingredients
225g oats
25g organic turmeric
5g ground black pepper
5g mixed herbs (oregano, thyme, rosemary, basil, mint, parsley)
25g mature cheddar cheese
50g raw organic coconut oil
Warm water to mix
Oat or spelt flour for rolling

Method

Preheat oven to 170ºC, 325ºF or Gas 3. Take a bowl and mix the oats, turmeric, black pepper, herbs and cheese. Warm the coconut oil, add it in the bowl along with enough water to bind it all together. Flatten out on a floured surface. Roll out to 1cm thickness and cut out into a size and shape fitting the size of dog you have (Eloise uses hearts roughly 5 × 5 cm for her 29kg greyhound.) Place on floured baking tray and bake for 15-25 minutes until done. Cool and then you can freeze them in layers of greaseproof paper in a sealed container. Depending on the size of the dog, I tend to break off a piece of biscuit and reward after a meal.

Golden Milk

This is another brilliant recipe to make for you and your dog: a delicious and very comforting digestive aid, with all the powerful anti-inflammatory and anti-oxidant properties of turmeric, minus the bitter taste. If your dog has stiff joints, try it daily for 30 days.

It will help with:

- Reducing inflammation
- Fighting bacteria
- Mopping up toxins in the body

- Clearing up itchy skin
- Improving digestion
- Deterring internal parasites
- Protecting against cancer
- Cleansing the blood

The main ingredient in golden milk is golden paste (or turmeric paste). This can easily be stored in the fridge for up to 30 days, or frozen in small amounts for up to three months, for use at a later date. Then you can make golden milk any time you like or as the need arises.

If you don't want to use cow's milk, make it with goat's milk (or Oatly is a good non-dairy option).

To make the golden paste:

Ingredients
120ml water
60g organic turmeric powder
70ml raw, organic coconut oil
1½ tsp freshly ground black pepper (a rare exception to my no-seasoning rule)

Method
Mix the water and turmeric in a small pan. Keep mixing on a medium heat until you have a thick paste. Keep a little extra water on standby in case it gets too thick. It won't

take two shakes to become a paste, so keep a watchful eye. Remove from the heat and mix in the coconut oil and pepper. Leave to cool. Store in an airtight container in the fridge for up to a month.

To make the golden milk:

Ingredients
240ml goat's milk, Oatly or almond milk, etc
turmeric paste*
1 tsp honey

> *Adjust the amount to suit the size of your dog: small dog: ¼ tsp, medium-sized dog: ½ tsp and large dog: ¾ tsp of paste.

Method
Heat the milk and stir in the turmeric paste and honey until dissolved. Pour some into your favourite Moomin mug for yourself. Give some to the dog in her bowl. Then, when you've finished yours, add the dog's share into your mug because she's such a princess she refuses to drink it from her bowl!

Food for Poorly Dogs

A lovely dinner for a dog who is off her food, courtesy of Eloise Walduck.

Ingredients
2 medium carrots, finely chopped
200g medium sweet potatoes, unpeeled and chopped
200g courgette or broccoli (or a mixture), grated
10g mixed herbs (oregano, thyme, rosemary, basil,
  mint, parsley)
150g cooked whole-grain or brown barley
50g organic raw coconut oil
500g venison, cut into strips

Method
Boil the carrots and sweet potato, and in the last five minutes of cooking time, add the courgette and/or broccoli. Once cooked, drain most of the liquid but leave some in the pan. Stir in the cooked barley, and the herbs. Add half the coconut oil and use a fork or potato masher to squish the sweet potato chunks to thicken the mixture. Set aside. In a non-stick frying pan add the other half of the coconut oil and gently fry the venison for approximately 5 minutes at low heat. Add some warm water to the pan, and let it simmer for a minute or two.

Add the venison along with its juice to the vegetable mix. Serve.

Chapter 5

Food supplements and functional foods

As we've seen, many health problems in dogs can be significantly relieved or eradicated entirely by changing over to a varied diet. A crucial part of the equation lies in adding functional foods or supplements to your pet's meals to make up for any vitamins and minerals that may be lacking.

A functional food is a product which has vitamins or something added to it, e.g. yoghurt containing probiotic, or dog treats with omega oil added.

A food supplement, on the other hand, is a vitamin or mineral which is eaten as a stand-alone addition, e.g. a probiotic supplement in tablet or powder form, or Yumega Plus – a fish oil preserved in such a way as to be mostly omega oils. Nikita, for instance, can't stand fish, so I add an omega oil blend to her dinner.

It's necessary to dedicate a chapter on food supplements and functional foods in this book because if you pick a winner it can have a transformative effect on your dog.

Conversely, select a dud and you may as well have bet on a horse you 'like the look of' in the 3.40 at Wincanton for all the good it will do. Just as with treats there are good, not-so-good and practically pointless options out there for you to spend your hard-earned cash on. I will try and shed a little light on how to make an informed decision.

Food supplements

To say that food supplements for animals are only lightly touched by regulation would be an overstatement. For example, a natural topical remedy for fleas has to be licensed, but when a food supplement purports to do the same job, it isn't checked over by any regulatory body. Which gives us both, lovely reader, a headache. Researching supplements has always proved tricky. I once had a trading standards officer tell me how confused he was about supplements for pets, even after all his enforcement training. So, for me, it comes down to these pointers. Look for:

- Brand
- Cost
- Word of mouth
- Customer service/communication

This humble list counts for a lot. Companies like Dorwest and Lintbells[9] put effort and resources into producing products that do what they say on the tin. And really that's all we want: a product that works. Crucially for a supplement to be effective, the active ingredient must be high-quality and available in the right amounts. Of course, high-quality ingredients cost money, so with supplements you generally do get what you pay for. Again, it's worth reading the ingredients label and avoiding the hype on the front of the box.

As a general rule, don't buy pet supplements from a supermarket as they won't be of great quality. And make sure you're buying supplements made for pets not humans. Our needs are different to a dog's, which are different to a cat's, and so on. Talk to your pet shop, find out what customers are coming back for again and again, ask questions on forums and get real advice. And call the manufacturer's customer service, if they've got one. Companies who are happy to chat through their products with you are more likely to have the dog at the heart of what they do.

Top tip: don't skimp on quality because you won't get the benefit. Don't waste a tenner on ordinary omega oils, buy tea and cake with that. Instead, spend £20 on phenomenal omega oils.

Supplements for the sick

If your dog has been on long-term steroids or antibiotics, or is receiving treatment you would like to stop, then adding supplements is definitely worth exploring. But don't just stop administering medication prescribed by your vet and switch overnight. Discuss it with your vet first and work out a plan for moving over gradually, if it's appropriate for your dog's condition. And please don't rely on well-meaning internet forum members as your sole advisors either. Or me, for that matter! Consult, consult, consult.

It's important to understand the side-effects supplements can have. A seaweed supplement could help keep Tilly's teeth clean, but if she suffers from hyperthyroidism, the iodine content in the seaweed could do more harm than good.

Did you know that St John's wort can increase bleeding during surgery and valerian can result in needing more anaesthetic?

I didn't either, but that's why doctors will always ask what herbal medicines you are taking before any operation. Supplements do work, but it's important to know in exactly what way, so that they alleviate as opposed to burden an already stressed body.

Supplements can also be taken alongside conventional, on-going treatment to help mitigate the effects medication may be having on your dog. You can feed a probiotic while giving antibiotics to offset the effect on the gut. You can give echinacea on a short-term basis to help a recovering dog, or one on long-term medication to keep their immune system up and fighting.

The market for supplements which target specific problems is growing rapidly too – stiff joints, poor digestion, fur loss, itchy skin and bad (dog) breath are all conditions that are well catered for.

When she first arrived as a rescue, Nikita had heinous dog breath, and really slimy saliva (I know, it's truly gross). After six months on a tiny scoop a day of CSJ Seaweed & Parsley supplement, I don't have to resist the urge to retch if I get a passing lick on the face when I'm sitting on the floor.

Treatments and supplements for every day

When you're talking about everyday maintenance it's much easier. Food supplements for fleas, ticks, mites, mange and worms are available and they work incredibly well. They've been working that way for thousands of years. It's only in the last 80 years or so that pharmaceutical parasite control has even existed. Before that it was nothing, or herbs. And the herbs *do* work.

I cover supplements and their uses in far greater detail in my book *Top Dog* and there is not enough room in here to digress from your dog's diet so I'll keep it brief by outlining my top hitters, as it were: the oils, lotions, liquids and herbs which really will give you bang for your buck.

Functional foods

Functional foods, otherwise known as nutraceuticals, are big business in pet food. They are foods, as I say, in which the health-giving supplements have already been added: glucosamine for joints; omega oils for heart health; essential amino acids L-tryptophan and L-carnitine for ageing dogs who are showing signs of dementia.

But, as with food supplements, quality really does count for something and it's important to know what you're looking for. Here are two things to bear in mind:

Check the other ingredients: Only buy a food or treat with a functional element if the other ingredients are good quality and not garbage. For example, I'm not going to give Nikita a dental chew containing cereals, derivatives, sodium tripolyphosphate (the active ingredients) and vegetable protein extracts. But I will give her a functional dental chew containing venison, seaweed (the active ingredient) and nothing else.

Pay attention to the order of the ingredients: As with all dog food, ingredients are listed by order of quantity – chicken 26%, barley 12%, salmon oil 2%, etc. The nutraceuticals in this list should come as an ingredient in their own right – e.g. omegas 3 & 6, glucosamine. And they should be listed above any minerals to stand a chance of being any use to your dog.

If you're unsure if a functional food or treat is worth its salt, talk to the producers and ask their advice. If they're not forthcoming, or you don't think the dog is at the heart of what they do, don't buy their products. A prime example of a good company is Feelwells[10], who produce probiotic dog treats. Feelwells do their research, the ingredients are good and the functional element is solid. All their treats are healthy and really do work. The probiotic treats were their first product and they're still going strong. Feed a couple of those a day and you won't be able to blame your own flatulence on the dog any more. Sorry!

Your shoe box of goodies

Here's a list of some great supplements to have on hand at all times. I've added these brands because I know they work very, very well, not because I sell them. Indeed, not all are on my website.

Product	What it's good for
Billy No Mates	Fleas, ticks, mites and mange
Four Seasons	Worms
Omega oils 3,6 & 9 Yumega Plus	Dry skin Moulting Itching and scratching from allergies
Virgin coconut oil (Biona Organic is good)	Improved skin, thyroid balance, better energy, weight loss
Unpasteurised apple cider vinegar – must be raw and contain 'mother'; I like Eden Nuganics	Arthritis, flea repelling, itchy skin, upset tummy settling
Joint Supplement Yumove	Stiff joints and improved mobility
Probiotic Yumpro	Probiotics to restore good gut health Restoring the gut after illness and medication Yeast overgrowth on skin and in ears
CSJ Seaweed & Parsley	Reduces plaque and tartar build up, reduces gum inflammation. Rich in Vitamins A and C, also minerals; potassium, iron and iodine.

Chapter 6

The diet plan

Putting together a diet plan that works for your dog isn't complicated, no matter how you choose to feed him – raw, cooked or shop-bought. As I've explained, the advantage of cooking for your dog or feeding raw is that the energy (or calorie) content is kept to a minimum, especially in comparison to commercial food, because he is getting fewer calories (and more nutrition) for the same volume. On the other hand, the majority of commercial pet food will (or should) contain all the vitamins and minerals necessary to make it a nutritionally complete food, which saves a deal of bother. (See p.53 for a refresher on what to look out for in good canned pet food).

What follows is my ideal feeding plan for my dog, Nikita. It's what works for us. You should follow it to the letter (I'm so kidding!). It's purely here to give you ideas, and the confidence to know that going off-piste and no longer opting for one food, every day, without deviation isn't going to harm your beloved. In fact it's going to do her shed-loads of good over the long term.

There's all sorts in here. Nikita gets her protein, vegetables, fruit and cereals from a whole host of great sources: lamb, chicken, offal, broccoli, carrots and corn, pears and apples, oats, rice and sweet potato, to name a few. And I don't worry about giving her raw chicken wings in the morning (which she adores more than anything else in the whole wide world) and then feeding her a cooked mince supper in the evening. To be honest, it's just as easy to cook up mince, sweet potato and green beans for her, the cat and myself. I just add more veg to mine and season it. When we're all having a night off she gets the best shop-bought wet food I can find (it's her equivalent of my takeaway). I never feed her kibble, or pasta.

I understand that my plan could look a bit labour-intensive and potentially expensive. I am aware, for example, that I live in a town (good access to supermarkets), in a house (space) with a freezer (chilly space) and you, lovely reader, may live an idyllic farmhouse existence, nestled in a mountain crevice (no supermarket, bags of space) or in a city flat (where you can get a beef carcass delivered on the back of a moped at midnight but have no space to hang it!) As I say, you must find a routine that suits your situation and lifestyle.

Before you start

Have your dog checked over by the vet. Get her weighed

and if the vet thinks there is weight to lose, discuss how much and at what rate you're aiming to lose it. Also make sure there are no underlying health issues, which might be exacerbated by your dog changing her diet and taking on more exercise.

Remind me of that weight loss formula again?

If your dog needs to lose weight, eating 15% less food is the magic number. That's 15% less in total, and not a consecutive figure. For example; if your 12kg dog usually eats 400g of food per day, a reduction of 15% would bring that down by 60g, leaving 340g required daily.

These figures are approximate. If you don't know how much you usually feed your dog, simply dole her food out as usual and weigh it before giving it to her. Start feeding her a varied diet and if her weight goes up a little, rein it in. If it drops too fast (more than 3-5% of bodyweight per month), feed more.

If your dog doesn't have a weight issue there are still great health benefits to be gained from getting her to start eating this way.

How long should my dog be on the diet?

I've made this an eight-week plan but this is an approximate figure: your dog will need several weeks on any new regime in order for you to be able see measureable changes and benefits. I've only listed two weeks' worth of meals below. That's because you're going to be cooking in bulk and there's no need for eight weeks' worth of separate recipes. The thinking is, by the time you've reached the end of the first fortnight, you should have enough frozen meals, and new food knowledge, to plan the next six weeks on your own, or simply repeat the two-week plan again, drawing on the food you've already prepared in the freezer. There is enough variety in the two weeks specified to make it balanced.

Also, once two weeks are up you will be starting to get a pretty clear picture of what your dog likes and doesn't like. Don't lose patience straight away and chuck out anything eyed with suspicion. My top tip is to put the food down and wander off; if you hover, your dog will know something's up and get suspicious. If the food is not gone within a couple of days, then yes, pollock, sweet potato and broccoli may not be up Oscar's alley. But only time, and trial and error, and not allowing yourself to be bent to the will of your dog, will tell.

A word on water

Put down fresh clean water at least twice a day. The water here in Sussex is really chlorinated so I filter mine and use it for everything, including the dog and cat. Clean, fresh water helps detox the body and flush out those kidneys.

What about treats?

All your dog's daily food intake needs to be taken into consideration. If you give him a couple of treats before bedtime, for example, you need to include them in his whole day's food allowance. Remember, this is a marathon, not a sprint. If your dog looks like he's putting on a bit, or not losing any, ask yourself, 'Does his bum look bigger than it did last week, or is that new T-shirt I bought him just not doing him any favours!'

Walkies!

The truth is that if you are taking in too many calories, you have to do a huge amount of exercise to compensate – and the same goes for your dog. That said, exercise does have an impact on how efficiently we burn the calories we take in, and it is absolutely key when it comes to overall wellbeing. It's no good having a slim dog if he's not a happy dog. So forgive me for being blunt about this: if you have a dog, you have to walk it. More than once a day. Fine if you've hired someone reliable to take your dog out (though by doing that you're missing out on so much), but make sure it happens.

When you've got a dog, going out should be built in to your every day, no matter what the weather's doing. Come hell or high water! And, trust me, as soon as you're out there working up a bit of a sweat, Mabel bounding in the grass, you'll both be the better for it.

Walking isn't just about exercise. It allows your dog to socialise with other dogs, which is essential to your dog's behavioural patterns. Reading the PDSA Animal Welfare (PAW) report's section on this saddens me deeply. It states that 54% of puppies never get any structured socialisation or training, or walks – 54%!

Let me break this down. Just as kids learn social behaviours by interacting with other kids in the playground, puppies need to get out, learn to play with other dogs and understand how to conduct themselves in public. In the park, older dogs teach younger dogs how to behave; and socialised dogs show un-socialised dogs (e.g. rescue dogs) how to get around town without being bullied or attacked – very important if you're to have a confident, independent dog.

The PAW report goes on to state that, 'A staggering 2.4 million dogs in the UK are not given the opportunity to exercise off the lead outside the home or garden on a daily basis. And 250,000 never go for walks at all! Quite apart from the life lessons the dog is missing out on, I think we can all agree it's incredibly cruel to keep a dog cooped up.

For those dogs that do go on walks, 81% are walked for less than an hour. Guilty? Then, let me reassure you that even the smallest change in a dog's exercise routine can make a significant difference to both your lives.

Apart from the socialisation side of things, the mental stimulation your dog gets by sniffing pavements, benches, walls, lampposts and grass, anywhere other dogs and animals have been is extraordinary. A 20-minute walk, especially on a new route around the block, can blow their tiny minds. Despite appearances, when you're on a walk, your dog isn't just sniffing away in the idle hope of finding a delicious morsel of cheese that's dropped out of somebody's sandwich (although that's certainly true some of the time…). Instead, he's picking up a whole host of nasal clues and marking his territory. I call it pee-mail. Who was here last? *pee* Who's trying to muscle in on my patch? *pee* That creep, George the Jack Russell's been out again, I'm not having *that* on our gate post *pee* Nirvana didn't come up with the song title 'Territorial Pi--ings' all on their own.

Excuses for why a dog isn't being walked properly range from the pathetic to the ridiculous (and I'm not pointing fingers here, I'm a culprit myself), but the one I hear most often is: 'I can't let him off, he'll never come back'. If you can't get your dog to come back when he's called then you *both* need training. It's important to teach recall, so I'd recommend going to a dog training class no matter how old you both are. The behaviours which make your dog run away are prompted by being on a lead all the time; he feels stifled. We wouldn't dream of keeping toddlers permanently in one of those child walking harnesses in the park: they wouldn't exercise properly or learn to play well with other kids if we did. And they wouldn't wear themselves out either. If your dog can't get a run-about, it's no wonder he barks so much or is constantly ripping up your plants. And being able to run about the house and garden, even if he is small, is not enough.

How much exercise?

The type of dog you have will determine how much exercise he needs. Until 2004, we had a gorgeous rescue lurcher, darling Bud, who would happily run about for an hour in the morning then take up residence on the sofa or, conveniently, in the hallway so you had to step over him every time you wanted to pass, for the rest of the day. And, if it was raining, good luck getting him out the door for a pee. Wasn't happening. He needed exercise, but not an inordinate amount, whereas Judy, our Jack Russell, needed running practically in to the ground!

No one knows your dog better than you do. A tired dog is a happy dog (and generally a well-behaved one, too). And if there's nothing physically wrong with him he needs a minimum of 30-60 mins exercise a day. That includes small breeds.

While you're following the diet plan, aim for five minutes more today than you did yesterday. When you're on the way home you want the dog lagging behind you, tired out. Or split it into three short walks; one before work, another with the dog walker, then the last one before dinner, or late evening.

Full disclosure: my chief excuse for not walking Nikita is: 'It's Sunday, we all need a day of rest.' Pathetic. But luckily for me we have a lovely little park up the road from the house which – with a twirl around the playing field, bowling green and churchyard – can be more than enough for us all on a wintry Sunday. But she has to have something.

Don't be a dog owner who never walks their dog. That's just cruel. Treat your dog and the responsibility of caring for her with respect. Sermon over. Now get your trainers on; you're going out.

Kate's No 1 Optimum Diet Plan for a Happy, Healthy Dog

Week 1

No raw DIY this week; we're starting gently with shop-bought food and home-cooked. Cooked leftovers can be frozen for another day.

Day One
Breakfast and dinner – Homemade Pork and Potato Stew
Treats – Apple slices

Lots of fresh water, and exercise (build in time for sniffing trees)

Day Two
Breakfast and dinner – Homemade Salmon and Vegetable Fishcakes
Treats – Shop-bought Billy & Margot strawberry and banana treats

Exercise!

Day Three
Breakfast and dinner – Homemade Simple Lamb
  Dinner
Treats – Homemade Liver Cake

You know what comes next – walks and tree sniffing

Day Four
Breakfast – Homemade Chicken Salad with Cottage
  Cheese
Dinner – Shop-bought Natural Instinct Country
  Banquet raw food
Treats – Uncooked broccoli and carrot pieces

Walkies!

Day Five
Breakfast – Shop-bought Natural Instinct Country
  Banquet raw food
Dinner – Homemade Fish Friday (doggy style!)
Treats – A couple of Feelwells probiotic lamb treats

You've got Eastenders on series record; round the
block you both go.

Day Six
It's the weekend! (Assuming you started your new
regime on Monday.) Leftovers, or something from the
freezer are the order of the day.

Breakfast – Whatever's left of the Natural Instinct
Dinner – More fish pie
Treats – Shop-bought Skippers fish bites

A big fat walk – at the beach, in the park, or the countryside. Find yourself a nice cafe or pub at the end of it and treat yourself.

Day Seven
Breakfast – Shop-bought Arden Grange Lamb and Rice wet food
Dinner – Either something you have made that day for next week's dinners or the rest of the Arden Grange

Treats – A juicy raw bone from the butcher

Week 2

We're going to put in a little raw food you've made yourself this week...

Day One
Breakfast and dinner – Homemade Raw Turkey Dinner
Treats – Billy & Margot treats

Don't forget that walk...

Day Two
Breakfast and dinner – Shop-bought Canagan wet food, any flavour you like
Treats – Natural Instinct Beef Pipe

Day Three
Breakfast and dinner – Homemade Fancy Chicken Dinner
Treats – Feelwells Venison Stick

Day Four
Breakfast and dinner – Homemade Raw Boneless Burgers
Treats – Feelwells Venison Stick

Day Five
Breakfast and dinner – Homemade Fancy Chicken Dinner (to use up what you have kept in the fridge)
Treats – Natures Menu Freeze-dried Rabbit Treats

Day Six
Breakfast and dinner – Shop-bought Raw Natures Menu Chicken and Tripe Dinner
Treats – Natures Menu Freeze-dried Rabbit Treats

Day Seven
Breakfast and dinner – Homemade Chicken Salad
  with Cottage Cheese
Treats – Fancy Eggs

Last orders

Hopefully this diet plan hasn't left you running around the house like a headless chicken, flinging open cupboards in search of a long-lost blender. Or heading for the recycling, book in hand, to bury it under half a dozen empty dog food tins. If the minimum you do is start to vary the shop-bought food and treats your dog gets – swapping low-quality dog food for higher-quality food based on the ingredients list and introducing variety by adding different flavours – you will be well on the way to giving your dog a healthier life.

If all your dog has ever known is poor-quality food and treats masquerading as the answer to your nutritional prayers, this change alone will reap huge rewards for both of you. Simply buying better dog food and watching your dog's weight will mean you have your dog for longer and they will be healthier.

The key to all this is having a bit of confidence to try new things, realising that as long as you stay off the banned foods list it's quite hard to poison your dog!

If you're cooking or feeding raw, use fresh food; don't

give them anything you wouldn't eat yourself because it's smelling a bit ripe; feed the same volume as you would normally pour from a dog food bag and see what occurs over the next few weeks. If they put on weight, reduce portion sizes. Don't give up at the first hurdle; you're not doing it wrong; you're just starting out and there are going to be ups and downs.

Within a couple of weeks you should see a difference in coat condition, energy levels and the state of their stools. After eight weeks, you should be able to refer back to the list of niggling problems that you made at the start of this book, and find that many of them – skin health, itching, dry coat, smells, weeping eyes and poor digestion – have improved dramatically. Don't be afraid to change things around. There is no right or wrong answer. It's whatever works for your dog. Some foods will agree with her, others won't. Some she just won't like; dogs have taste preferences just as we do. You'll soon find your groove.

Now go get started. Be brutally honest with yourself about your dog's weight and overall condition. Use the body conditioning score to work out just how much poop you're in, weight-wise, and get cracking.

Remember:
- Buy the best pet food you can afford
- Choose high-quality ingredients if you're doing it yourself
- Get out and exercise with your dog

If you can come back to me after eight weeks and tell me there's no improvement whatsoever – in weight, health, mood (that's the dog's *and* yours) – I'll eat dog food and put it online to prove it.

That's about it. Feed them right, watch them blossom. And start planning that holiday in the sun you can now afford because you're not spending it on your dog's long term medication. I'm thinking, Naples! G&T anyone?

Endnotes

1   https://www.pdsa.org.uk/what-we-do/annual-reviews
2   https://www.animalsciencepublications.org/publications/jas/article
    s/90/5/1653?highlight=&search-result=1
3   http://circres.ahajournals.org/content/96/9/939.full
4   https://www.animalsciencepublications.org/publications/jas/article
    s/90/5/1653?highlight=&search-result=1
5   http://www.vcahospitals.com/main/pet-health-information/article/
    animal-health/brachycephalic-airway-syndrome-in-dogs/2143
6   http://www.ncbi.nlm.nih.gov/pubmed/18635428
7   http://www.ncbi.nlm.nih.gov/pubmed/21486641
8   http://www.ncbi.nlm.nih.gov/pubmed/21486641
9   Look them up at www.dorwest.com and www.lintbells.com
10 www.feelwells.co.uk

Further feeding

Shop-bought complete raw food and treats
Your local pet shop!
Natural Instinct – www.naturalinstinct.com
Nutriment – www.nutriment.co.uk
Natures Menu – www.naturesmenu.co.uk
Basil's Dog Food – www.basilsdogfood.co.uk

Bespoke raw food tailored to your dog
Honey's Real Dog Food – www.honeysrealdogfood.com

Raw DIYers
Your local butcher, should you be lucky enough to still have one
Morrisons – unusual cuts of meat, always British, inexpensive
Lidl – British, inexpensive. Do good frozen fish too

Online bulk buy raw food retailers
www.landywoods.co.uk
www.thedogsbutcher.weebly.com
www.wolftucker.co.uk
www.rawtogo.co.uk

Shop-bought cooked dog food
The list is longer than you think, but here are some winners: Nature Diet, Natures Menu, Arden Grange, Barking Heads, Forthglade, Natures Harvest, Applaws. Talk to your local pet shop or go online www.thedog-diet.co.uk for more information.

Further reading

Read
Raw Meaty Bones by Tom Lonsdale

Avail yourself of expert online knowledge:
www.thedogdiet.co.uk
www.rawstartexplained.webs.com
www.dogfoodadvisor.com
www.petforums.co.uk
www.dogster.com

Acknowledgements

I am the kind of writer who needs a gun to her head to meet a deadline. It's essential that I moan about how hard it is to write a book, even though it's such a privilege to get the chance in the first place, until good friends tell me to shut up and get on with it. To them I say this:

Thanks Victoria Marshallsay for your optimism, support and giving me a good talking to when I need it. Thanks to Amber, my brilliant and glamorous assistant for keeping everything else afloat while I typed (and whined continually) in the corner for months.

Special thanks to Martin Dunford who, to my eternal shame, I forgot to thank when I wrote the first book. Bad friend! Martin, you're an amazing mate. Thanks for all your help and support.

Thanks also to vet Nick Thompson for your honesty and help. I enjoyed sparring with you over kibble as dog food immensely! And to a pet food consultant who wishes to remain nameless for opening my eyes.

A very large dose of thanks and my heartfelt gratitude to Richard Allport for reading the book and writing such a kind and generous foreword.

To Simon Collyer as always, all my lovely My Itchy Dog customers and my vet Ciara Murphy.

Thanks again go to Short Books, especially Aurea 'I now cook for my dog' Carpenter, Klara 'just one more thing' Zak and Rebecca Nicolson for keeping the doggy faith and asking for another book.

And last but never, ever least, Toni Basset for being 'spectacular'. Love you, Marcus!

Index

Author biography

Kate Bendix worked for many years in
television documentaries. In 2009, she jacked it all
in, embraced poverty and started her own business,
My Itchy Dog. Being an experienced broadcaster
and journalist, she still loves the sound of her own
voice and features on radio shows and in dog
magazines whenever she can get past security.
She lives by the sea.